The First Seven Towers Anthology
First published 2008
By
Seven Towers Agency,
4, St Mura's Terrace,
Strangford Road,
East Wall,
Dublin 3,
Ireland.

www.seventowers.ie

ISBN Perfect Bound Edition 978-0-9555346-7-6

Book design concept by Solid Design
www.soliddesign.ie
Cover, artwork, type and layout design and typesetting by
Seven Towers Agency
www.seventowers.ie

Printed by Betaprint, Ireland.
Printed on 90gsm Muncken Bookwove White.

A SEVEN TOWERS PUBLICATION

Preface

The performance of literary word is a very significant part of writing throughout the world, from *seanachaí* and tribal story tellers, through to performance poets and one person shows. Listening to a literary work performed aloud is a very different experience to reading it in one's own time anonymously on the page. Though each is different, they are both important and it is necessary and right that they exist side by side as part of the one overall process of literary communication.

The purpose of this anthology is to reflect both these traditions side by side and, for that reason, all writers featured in this anthology, bar one, read at a Seven Towers event or an event in which Seven Towers writers took part. The one exception was Ray Pospisil who sadly died before most of us could hear him read in person. His work though, was first introduced to Ireland through the open mic scene in Dublin, where it was read by Ray's good friend Quincy R Lehr.

We at Seven Towers hope that this will be the first of many print collaborations with the spoken word.

Seven Towers,

November 2008.

Introduction

This introduction is taken from a speech given by Ross Hattaway at the Poetry Spring Festival in Lithuania in May 2008.

Universal literacy is a very recent phenomenon in most cultures. Accordingly, the act of reading is a curious beast and it takes more than one form. In a literate world, it can be solitary — we read to and for ourselves. We can use reading as a shared experience, in reading to children or in a community of readers, reading the same texts on recommendation because someone tells us that we simply must read this or that. We can also invite and involve an audience and they, in listening, are part of that act of reading. For the relatively short part of human history that has been accompanied by written texts, normal participation in reading for the vast illiterate majority of our ancestors was as an audience.

From the second half of the twentieth century, it is the first of these, the solitary reading of texts, which has predominated in literate societies. This is hardly surprising. Literacy gave access to information and this gave the literate enormous status and power – political, secular, spiritual and, of course, economic – and much of this power had to be given on trust by the illiterate, which is always the most enduring grant of authority. As more and more of us gained access to something that was previously the preserve of the elite, it was only normal that we would seek the most prestigious form of this skill and that we would begin to abandon the particular participation that had marked us as outside that elite, that of the listening audience. In more totalitarian regimes in the early and mid twentieth century, that is within living memory, literacy was not quite the issue — the written word implied official approval and the written word came weighed with implied authority and, ultimately, the power of the state.

That reading gives pleasure appears self-evident. We only need to see the joy of being read to in small children, or the hunger for the inner life of the imagination in older children as their reading keeps pace with their developing sense of self and other and gives them clues as to how this world and those in it may work. It is no accident, it would seem, that so much of writing for children is condensed and rhythmic — in short, poetry. However, it is also evident that many people in later life do not enjoy reading, in particular reading poetry. Why is this so?

One possible answer lies in the manner in which we rose into literacy, whereby higher status has been accorded to one type of reading – the solitary experience of being alone with a text – over other forms. The reader, after early childhood, rarely experiences poems as anything other than a written text. The way that we are brought to poetry through education disconnects the types of reading and never re-joins them. It is this separation of the strands of reading that is the central problem. It is difficult to imagine a world where songs would not be listened to or sung, but read as texts on a page, yet this is how poems are presented, are seen and read. A core part of the writing process, of an actual audience, is not available to writers and an equally large part of the innate pleasure of being a reader is denied to readers.

As in theatre, as in music, being an audience is an act of trust – if there is no need for audience, there is no need for trust. Poets who deny their need for physical audience risk, in the long term, losing the trust of their readers, that act of faith that this is something worthwhile and worth having in their lives, that the writer is passionate about readers and about how they read. If that is the case, it is little wonder, then, that we have so many adults in a highly educated nation who do not gain pleasure from reading poetry, when the reading of poetry was their first step in the whole adventure.

Paul Casey

Paul coordinates publishing, book launches, tours, workshops and readings. He also emcees the weekly poetry open-mic, Ó Bhéal. A poet himself, Paul has also lectured in screenwriting in both Dublin and South Africa. The following article *Reading your poetry* was written by Paul.

Reading your poetry

Much has been said about lack of projection, caesura, enunciation and so forth, which are all very important for compelling delivery. I often encourage poets to take their work to the ears of the world, and thankfully far less frequently, urge others to keep theirs at home, for some short consideration at least. It's never a good idea to openly read poetry just because one has written it. It needs to be ready for the world too, to confidently ring with an empathy as in storytelling, dramatics aside. Reading it too soon is akin to publishing prematurely. Many who poet on the open-mics and at formal readings spend moons incubating and crafting their work. It's only the miraculous minimum that never needs it, to be fair.

Voicing poetry openly is by no means void of reward, unless you're looking for a new car, a new ego perhaps. Yet you still need to get it out there. Now staple to a forest tree trunk an ad for your favourite missing pen. It's soon lost along with the sound of the falling tree, and may just as well be attached to it. How many voices will never be heard? It's daunting in the beginning for any poet to bare their all, though oftentimes addictive soon after. For some, reading their verse to an audience is mere therapy. Others pursue the candid, uncertain spotlights of affirmation and evaluation. For many it's simply art. Whichever way, it wants to be grasped, so it's worth taking the time to listen to one's own elocution, to sound the poetry as fluently as possible, and to not rely on the composition alone.

Public readings and performances often present a gamut of fibre and *filí*, from the extremely personal to the coldly objective — from the atrociously painful or simply boring to the deeply enlightening, shocking or spectacular, and to as profound as the turning of the old cauldron itself. They can irreversibly catalyse a personal revolution within a single gesture. Reciting re-awakens the poet's initial dialogue, opening it to more ears, each with new and differing shades of discernment. It creates an open space for reflection on the collective experience in a time when deception and paramnesia are more rife than ever. It transcribes the personal poetic canvas into the common sky for all to see and hear. And above all for me, it is the art of *gift-giving*, through the most complex form of communication we have.

On this altruistic note, the poet is the educator, filling in the gaps as it were, left by an impersonal matrix of theory. Live poetry gives immediate access to direct experience, thus expanding horizons and perceptions, by way of example, and helping to reverse the enduring concussions of traditional pedagoguery. It reverberates with our ability to remain humane, making salient the values that crumble about us every day and nourishing them for the patient and receptive. It does this organically and in a way that any attempt at preaching is immediately suspended for critical digestion. Demagogues haven't a hope here, and politicians usually walk out red-faced.

Once poetry is published, in a sense ownership is lost into the public domain, and every successive visual reading of it will fashion a new interpretation, seldom returning to the poet. Reading it is a way of retaining that ownership. Each poem grows and becomes more a part of the poet when read aloud, as younger reds should be decanted to release the tannin-locked flavours. Poets who recite their work without the page have a far more complete ownership of it than those who do, and their delivery is usually many shades richer. Reading it directly from the page can be just as effectual though if practiced adequately, to liberate the intended emphases and subtleties not always evident in script. Listeners are more receptive to its nuances. The verse becomes more colourful within the realms of immediate response, and breathes in a way it could not while resting between the long-considered pages of an exclusive editorial. The poet and poem are seen then as a single, living signature.

Reading poetry challenges our fellow humans to fly with us, and the sky is begging for our most eloquent efforts. So preen those feathers! Whatever the composition, try to deliver it with the authority it deserves and the passion with which it was formed. Our eyes and ears await!

Kevin Higgins

Kevin Higgins was born in London, but grew up in Galway city. His collections are *The Boy With No Face* (Salmon, 2005) and *Time Gentlemen, Please* (Salmon, 2008). With his wife Susan Millar DuMars, he organises the *Over The Edge* readings in Galway. A collection of his reviews and essays, *Poetry, Politics and Dorothy Gone Horribly Astray* (Lapwing), was published in 2006. He is the poetry critic of the *Galway Advertiser* and also regularly reviews for *Books In Canada: the Canadian Review of Books.* He lives in Galway. The folowing article *Tomorrow Belongs To Us,* is by Kevin.

Tomorrow Belongs To Us

Until the 1990s there was, for most, no way to be a poet in Ireland and not be opposed to things as they were. The Irish feminist movement of the 1970s and 80s had its poetic counterpart in Eavan Boland's 1982 collection *Night Feed* (Arlen House); the Catholic church was pretty wickedly satirised in poems such as Paul Durcan's "Priest Accused of Not Wearing Condom" and the brave new Ireland of the late 1970s was starkly taken to task in poems such as "Cuchulainn" by Michael O'Loughlin: "At eleven-fifteen on a Tuesday morning / with the wind blowing fragments of concrete / Into eyes already battered and bruised / By four tightening walls / In a flat in a tower-block / Named after an Irish Patriot / Who died with your name on his lips..."

Suffering poverty is one thing; poets have a long history of being fairly okay with poverty, both their own and other people's. But living under the then very real yoke of the Catholic Church — the constitutional ban on divorce, homosexual acts between consenting men illegal until 1993, the sale of condoms completely illegal until 1979 — was bound to provoke opposition from artists. I think it was Trotsky who wrote that "artists are petit-bourgeois in revolt against the role society is trying to force them into", or words to that effect. Until at least the late 1970s all Irish writers had to worry about censorship; and Irish women writers had to constantly fight against the silence which had been imposed on their mothers and grandmothers. In the Ireland of the recent past if you were a poet, or artist of any sort, what you were *for* may not have been at all clear; but you typically knew what you were against.

In the past 20 years, many of these issues have either ceased to be or been greatly ameliorated. The church is nothing like the force it was. Censorship is a distant abstraction to young writers starting out now. These days a poet is far more likely to draw the wrath of the Left for not toeing some 'party line' than he or she is to be condemned by the powers that be, who are, to be frank, so secure in their position of ideological supremacy that they don't care what poets say about them. Yes, free market capitalism has, with impunity, put its hands into pretty much every area of Irish life over the past decade or so. Most artistic types don't like this, or at least think it has gone too far. But they are not alone in not having a clue what is to be done about it.

Voting for Enda Kenny (with a bit of Eamonn Gilmore thrown in) seems unlikely to change much. And to the bulk of artists, as to most people, the existing far Left seems to be more about the past than the future. Even the most apolitical poet knows about what Stalin did to artists and no-one wants to revisit that. Those few who do loudly engage with political issues tend to follow the formula of writing a stream of vituperative letters to the editor (everywhere from the *Irish Times* to the *Longford Independent*) in which they often conclude by sniping at their fellow scribes for not being similarly engagé. For most, excepting those tragic few on the far Left who are impressed, it is clear that this sort of 'political engagement' is more about death than life. 'Notice me!' the sad scribe shrieks, 'Before they screw down my coffin lid'. But the world has more important things to attend to. And so the scribe shrieks all the louder. The value of the political engaged writer has rarely been more open to question than in Ireland right now.

In this context, Dave Lordan's explosion onto the Irish poetry scene over the past couple of years has been a revelation. In his poetry, Lordan is open about his politics; his point of view is usually that of participant rather than bystander, as in the case 'Migrant's March, Genoa, July 19, 2001':

The slogans surging up the back of fifty thousand throats
to greet them in our provisional republic.

> Free-Free Kurdistan.
> So-So Solidarité.
> A- Anti- Anti-capitalista.
> Un altro mondo é possible.
> Noi siamo tutti clandestini.

A language we all understand.
Is there any such thing as Ireland?

The closing couplet well brings to life the way participation in big political movements can help us transcend the apparently commonsense realities around us. The experimental five page 'Excerpt from Reflections on Shannon' & 'The hunger striker sings his death' also both overtly engage with politics in a way that your typical poet believer in all things Irish Times would not:

from 'Excerpt from Reflections on Shannon'

> I ask you again
> What the fuck is silence;
> And who ever heard
> The dead requesting it?

I have, on occasion, heard Lordan's poems criticised for being somewhat bombastic and more than a little relentless. It's important to know that Lordan considers the 'stage' i.e. reading his poems aloud to an audience, to be more important than the page i.e. having his poems quietly read from a book by solitary passive readers. When he is on form, he is one of the best performers Irish poetry has to offer. I once saw him perform 'The hunger striker sings his death' to a Galway audience which included a woman from a protestant unionist background in the North, who up to that point had more or less believed that the H-Block hunger strikers were just a bunch of guys who had starved themselves to death years ago to make some obscure political point. After the reading, this same woman turned to me and said: "Now I get it." As a poet, Lordan has an ability to animate a subject in a way that far outstrips most of even the better public speakers on the Left.

There have, yes, been one or two old guarders keen to pour ignorant scorn on the open-mic and poetry slam scene which has sprung up in most of the key urban centres in Ireland over the past five years: they are the sort of people who would no doubt amend Yeats's exhortation to future generations of Irish poets from "Irish poets, learn your trade" to 'Younger poets, know your place'. A professor of Irish-Studies based at a major American university, a pillar of the literary establishment, if you will, recently likened the aforementioned naysayers to those old men who like to whinge away to themselves about how "there's never anything any good on the telly these days!"

In Ireland the tradition of poetry, the spoken art is particularly strong. According to the *Oxford Companion to Irish Literature*:

When Lady Gregory and Yeats were gathering folk material in Co. Galway in 1897 and thereafter, they encountered many stories about [Anthony] Reaftearai (1779-1835) and found that his poems were still sung and recited.

Reaftearai was illiterate, and his poems were never written down during his lifetime.

As the 19 century moved on, Irish poetry found a home in the Victorian drawing room. Reaftearai reciting his verses to peasant ne'er-do-wells gave way to Mister Yeats reciting his poems to small gatherings of old dears, and not-so-old dears, pausing between stanzas to sip tea from a bone china cup.

Lately, what Dave Lordan calls "the live poetry movement" has energised the poetry reading scene by reconnecting Irish poetry with its own oral tradition. At the Over The Edge: Open Readings in Galway City Library, there are featured readers with an open-mic afterwards. Many well known poets have been featured readers: the likes of Dennis O'Driscoll, Medbh McGuckian and Colette Bryce. But the democratic element which a properly structured open-mic introduces has been crucial to the event's success. Several poets who began at the open-mic have gone on to be featured readers. A similar openness is also crucial to poetry slams and other new reading series, such as O'Bhéal in Cork and the White House readings in Limerick, both of which encompass an open-mic. The old style, non-inclusive poetry reading, with its small audience and reverential attitude to the one established poet reading will soon, all the signs are, be a thing of the past. Tomorrow belongs to us.

Liam Aungier

Liam is a poet from Co Kildare. He was twice runner up in the Patrick Kavanagh poetry competition. His debut collection *Apples in Winter* is published by Doghouse Books. The following three poems are by Liam Aungier.

Hide and Seek

I was off the ground. Careful
Not to snap its branches,
I was climbing up,
Scuffing my Sunday shoes to ascend
Into its bell of foliage.
A spider scrambled across my hand,
Twigs tangled in my hair. I was
Rooted there, entirely alone, entirely
At one with the world, no longer
Myself, I was half feral,
Hearing as a bird might hear,
A tractor stuttering into voice,
A farm-dog barking across two fields -
Until my brothers came calling me,
Calling me back to my name.

The Light of Delft

from the painting "Woman Writing a Letter with her Maid" by Jan Vermeer

Nothing here is happening. The servant girl
Is standing still by the leaded window,
Arms folded. Her mistress sits expressionless
Behind a covered table. Just now her quill
Has ceased scratching on the handmade paper.
The morning waits...

Only the light is happening. Dispersed,
It sparkles from the silver writing set,
Defines the volume of a starched white sleeve,
It is refracted, reflected, it illuminates
Five panels of stained glass, finds out
The lady's diamante broach, a pearl earring.
The one true subject of all your art, Vermeer,
This resplendent, this empirical light of Delft.

The Meaning of Snow

"Isn't there some meaning?"
"Look out there... It's snowing. What's the meaning of that?"
—   Chekhov, *Three Sisters.*

Snow is a white rose
Shedding its million petals
On the naked earth.

Open your mouth
And it will settle on your tongue
Like a sacrament.

It loves places we
Disregard, it rests on roofs,
On walls, in gutters.

Rain drips and splashes
In its loud downpour, but snow
Falls without a sound.

It is a memory
Of half-forgotten mornings
Of my boyhood.

Through the hours of night
Even when no-one watches
Still it falls and falls.

It makes the earth new,
Cold and white and alien.
The moon is its sister.

It too is mortal.
The T.V. news has promised
Rain before dawn. So

Let us go out now:
We might discover bird-tracks
Written on the snow.

Eamon Carr

Eamon is a significant figure in the Irish artistic and cultural scene for many years. In the late 1960s, he co-founded Tara Telephone, the music and poetry group of the Dublin beat scene. Following on from Tara Telephone, in the 1970s Eamon co-founded Horslips, the hugely influential band which is credited with creating the musical genre known as Celtic Rock, and in which he is also a drummer, conceptualist and lyricist. Eamon has also promoted musicians and artists, and works as a journalist, writer and commentator on culture, politics, arts, music and sport, as well as being an award-winning broadcaster. He was born in Co. Meath and lives in Dublin. His first collection *The Origami Crow, Journey into Japan World Cup Summer* 2002 is published by Seven Towers. The next two poems are by Eamon Carr.

Bob Collins And His Sailin' Shoes

I'm sure there could have been memories more profound
But, as the eulogies were being read at your funeral,
I saw you,
Years earlier,
Chasing a frisbee in St. Stephen's Green.

Rushing across the grass,
Arms outstretched,
Reaching heavenwards in sweet ecstasy,
A supplicant in a Titian's Assumption.

Smiling
And laughing,
At one with the moment,
You seemed in harmony with all things.

Chance had me back in that public park again
The day after your cremation.

Along the leafy nave near Dawson Street,
I walked briskly,
As if to outstrip the sadness which shadowed me.

Nearby,
A man and a child strolled past the pond.
He inhaled from a cigarette and, rock show in miniature,
A cloudy continent of bright smoke
Broke spectacularly around his head in a saintly blue halo.

Then,
As I gazed admiringly,
Torn by the breeze,
It scattered,
Slowly, deliberately, delicately,
Into the uttermost reaches of the universe.

somewhere in liverpool

somewhere in liverpool
she makes stuffed toys
for kids in an orphanage.

I met her in a burger bar
when I was coming down.

she started a conversation.

she talked of family she
never knew

and how she was always busy
coming up to christmas.

she had a companion who,
as I recall,
cried a lot.

saying "goodbye and
happy christmas"
I left her,
cramped by the window
as,
outside,
lovers met

fortified on carbohydrates
I went to an evening
football match.

Tom Conaty

Tom is a Dublin based poet and teacher originally from Cavan. For the past thirty years he has worked with the Arts in Education, focusing particulary on poetry in Primary Education. A member of The Board of Poetry Ireland, he has been an advisor to the Arts Council and regular contributor to RTE literary programmes. Published widely, his first collection is due out soon.

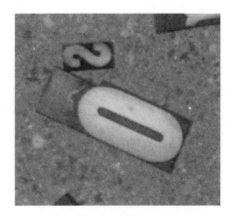

Calling

Of a sudden
unannounced
like the spoor
of a hare
on dew

On a morning
when possibilities
seem pure
and something
is calling...

Wintering

The wind is coming
from a different direction now –
stops the river
flowing.
bids the waterfall stand
still.

in flight the geese
undo their V,
and even the night owl
cannot see

the arched and stiffened whitethorn
straightening, taking in air from
a different course,
its source, a mouth-opening place
between here and there,
now and then.

parchment of white, scrolls back
on the stricken birch,
inviting us to read
the manuscript beneath...

Where are the Mourners

Where are the mourners now
That this day is done,
Drawing to a close on this union
That was ours.

Sufficient light no more to see,
To walk side by side,
Senses dimmed by the cackle
And squawk of scheduled time, gone.

But when all is said and done,
It's down to the arc
Of an opening
And closing door,

The passage through,
The dare not look back
Moment of —
Going

The latch,
Click-clacking behind,
And the unmistakable sound
Of   shut.

Flagstone of granite,
Two steps,
Down a path and
Out a black garden gate.

An electric saw whines
its way through timber,
on a building site,
nearby

and somewhere,
autumn grass,
surrenders to the lawnmower's
blade.

Steve Conway

Dublin based Steve Conway is currently a DJ on Phantom 105.2FM and a former stalwart of that epic journey on that good ship that housed Radio Caroline. Steve's memoir about his time on Radio Caroline will be published by Liberties Press in March 2009. Steve's memoir gives us a behind the scene, fly on the wall look at the piece of cultural and broadcasting history that is Radio Caroline on its stormy journey through the 1980s until it ran aground at the end of that decade. The following true story is by Steve.

Old Haunt

By the autumn of 1991, the Ross Revenge was effectively a ghost ship, though not in the supernaturally accepted sense of the term.

New legislation introduced by the British Government at the end of 1990 had effectively silenced Radio Caroline, and no transmissions had been made from the vessel for a period of some 10 months. The law purported to give the British state the right to board, search and seize a ship, even in international waters, if they suspected that unlicenced radio transmissions were emanating from it. There was enough uncertainty in the way that the new law was worded to give Caroline considerable hope that a legal loophole could be found, so, while the lawyers went to work, the ship remained out at sea, but silent.

Just a skeleton crew were left on board, usually only 3 or 4 people, enough to keep it lit and to keep watch. The studios and corridors which had once echoed to music and the scurrying feet of busy DJs were empty and silent, the cabins where so many had lived and loved during the 80s were mostly unoccupied and in darkness. The main generators were shut down to conserve fuel, with a small one running to provide the legal minimum of lighting required on the bow and stern of the ship, as well as powering a TV, kettle, fridge, microwave and a limited number of very low wattage lightbulbs in the few remaining populated rooms and corridors. As the initial months of optimism when we expected a legal solution started to fade, little moved on board the ship, and it seemed as if both the fabric of the vessel and the Caroline organisation itself were in a state of decay.

If ever there was a time when we would have expected the fabled Ross Revenge ghost to show itself, this was it. Over the years, from the several hundred crew and DJs who had come and gone from the ship, there had always been tales of the ship's ghost, an unexpected presence when you were alone in the dark, unexplained footfalls on the bridge in the dead of night, a touch on the shoulder when there was no one there.

That someone had died on board the Ross Revenge, was a known fact, part of the history of the ship during its days as an Icelandic trawler, one of the mighty Grimsby fishing fleet that sailed in the frozen waters of the north for months on end in the 1960s. A crewmember had been killed, suddenly and horribly, literally cut in two when one of the huge steel trawl wires snapped under tension when hauling in the North Atlantic.

The days when the Ross Revenge had been the largest of the British fleet fishing off Iceland belonged not only in another time, but seemingly to another world. Documentary evidence, and stories from the men who sailed on the Ross fleet in those days – for it was all men – portrayed an incredibly harsh and cruel way of life, with 16 hour working days for months on end, mostly outdoors, and with considerable risk of injury. During the autumn of '87, we had been joined on Caroline by Ernie, a grizzled old Grimsby man, well into his 60s, who had formerly worked on board the Grimsby trawlers, including the Ross Revenge itself, in the '50s and '60s. The tales he told us of the conditions on board in those days were very sobering, and very different from the working conditions that would be allowed in our time. Men who were injured – and there was almost always someone injured on a trip – were not brought ashore, for the valuable fishing time could not be lost, and to divert hundreds of miles to land would mean financial loss for the owners. If you were injured, you were patched up by your colleagues on board, and lay in the ship's hospital cabin for however many days it took until the trip was over, and you could be brought to proper medical care ashore.

One of Ernie's relatives had died on one such trip in earlier years when injured and having to wait several days before landing for treatment. As if this tale was not bad enough, Ernie told us of an even darker side to those days — if you got injured on the trip, even on the last day, you did not get your bonus based on the size of the catch, and it was split out amongst everyone else who made it ashore safely. According to Ernie, if you didn't get on with your fellow crew members, you would need to be very careful in watching your back towards the end of a trip, lest a sudden and mysterious accident overcome you. Ernie well believed that the ghost of the dead fisherman could haunt the Ross Revenge, though we tried to persuade him that surely this spirit would find the more relaxed conditions on board now that it was a pirate radio ship to be more to his liking.

By the autumn of 1991 the skeleton crew consisted of myself and Neil Gates, the only former broadcasters left on board, a volunteer helper called Christian, and my girlfriend Wendy, who had agreed to spend some weeks out at sea with me. On the long autumn evenings as we reminisced about better times before Caroline had been silenced and the people we had worked on board with, the conversation sometimes turned to the ghost, but we had never experienced any manifestations ourselves, even now, surrounded as we were by empty rooms and dimly lit corridors. Such things were pure fantasy, we agreed — there were always enough noises on an old and creaking ship to make anyone with a fanciful imagination scared in the dark.

And so when, one morning, over breakfast, I told Neil and the others about a startlingly vivid dream I had had the night before, we were all, myself included, quick to dismiss it in jest as an encounter with our fictional ghost.

In the dream, I had walked into the galley to be confronted by a total stranger, an old, hard-bitten looking man, in working clothes and fisherman's overall. He didn't look like Ernie, but had the same Grimsby accent. He accosted me angrily.

"Layabout," he spat at me with some venom. "This was a working ship. Men worked her, real men, working hard. We worked here and we died here. And you lot — you come along with your radio station and all your fancy modern stuff and you defile it. You defile us. You with your music, your central heating and your fancy fluorescent lighting and women – you bring women on board! We had no heating, no fancy modern lights and we had no women on board this ship. You've been here long enough playing at your radio station and you can't even do that now and you are just living on board like useless layabouts. Well it's over. It's finished. This ship doesn't want you any more".

Neil and the others were in fits of laughter as I recounted this, and the general consensus was there there had been far too much cheese used in the pizzas that Neil had baked for us the night before. And then we finished our breakfast, and set about another day of minding our ghost ship, doing nothing, and waiting for the legal loophole that might never come.

Except, this was not quite like any other day on board the Ross Revenge.

This was to be the day that the central heating radiator in the messroom sprang a leak, destroying the carpet. This was the day in which Christian, our 6" 3' tall volunteer crewmember, forgot to duck when approaching the cooker in the galley, and split his forehead open by smashing his head into the low hung fluorescent light over the cooker. It looked worse than it was, there was a lot of blood, but the cut was minor.

And this was the night when Wendy, having fried an omelette in the frying pan left on the cooker after dinner, suddenly started bleeding from the mouth, and realised that the crunchy bits in the omelette she was eating were not pieces of eggshell that she had missed, but shards of glass from the smashed light.

The central heating, the fancy fluorescent lights, and the woman.

I never believed in the Ross Revenge ghost, and I can honestly say that my alleged encounter was only a dream.

But knowing the future can be worrying, and I've learned my lesson.

I'm staying the hell away from Neil's pizza in future.

Catherine Ann Cullen

Catherine Ann is a poet from Dublin. She is a regular contributor to RTE Radio 1's *Sunday Miscellany* and *A Living Word* as well as producing current affairs, arts and features. She lives with her partner Harry and daughter Stella in Kimmage, Dublin. Her first collection, *A Bone in My Throat*, is published by Doghouse Books in Kerry. Catherine Ann won the 2008 Francis Ledwidge Award. The next three poems are by Catherine Ann.

In Defence of Chocolate

Eating chocolate is not a sin,
And cakes cannot be wicked,
Whatever the magazines say.

Au contraire, oh éclair:
Eating chocolate is a religious experience,
Unless you covet your neighbour's chocolate
Or kill him for it.

Keeping chocolate is the opposite of a sin.
You can use it to honour your father and mother,
Share it with your neighbour and his wife.

Making chocolate mousse is a corporal good work
That feeds the hungry,
A spiritual good work that comforts the sorrowful.

You take three eggs
And 200 grammes of dark chocolate.
You need only 170 grammes
But the other thirty keep the cook virtuous.
Separate the eggs, and whip the whites
Till they are bright and stiff as archangels' wings,
Or billow white as summer-clouds,
Cumulo nimbus, floating close to heaven,
The kind that cherubs sit upon.

Melt the chocolate in a *bain marie.*
I like to think it's named for the Virgin Mary,
Because anyone who has had an immaculate conception
Can surely bathe without touching the water.

Beat your trinity of yolks into the chocolate,
And stir a little spirit in:
Brandy, cointreau, if you must, *Lacrimae Christi.*

Then, fold in the egg whites
Till you have God's good air
Trapped in a layer of chocolate.

As long as you're not too proud of it,
Your chocolate mousse will smooth your path to heaven,
Helping you to love your enemies,
And your neighbour as yourself.

Reines Claudes Dorees

We came to Beaugas in the
heatwave
To harvest your greengages
And found the *Reines Claudes
Dorees*
A queen's ransom in the trees.

I felt myself full of promise,
A life three weeks inside me
So new I told you only
To turn away your *eau de vie.*

On the orchard grass, bittersweet
windfalls,
Blown down before their time.
It had happened twice before:
But this time I felt fruitful, sure.

Between mornings and afternoons
of picking golden fruit
Leaping for high branches,
Stripping them almost bare,
We rested in the shade at noon.

I sat warm on a fallen tree
With my love, my friend, my friend's love, and my child-to-be,
With plums like sunshine bursting in my mouth
And thought, *This is enough.*

Sometimes the fruit was sticky.
Insects had got there first,
Their entrance marked by
A thin trickle of honey.

And though we kept the plums overnight
Cool as the baking dark allowed
Their bloom had lost a shade by
morning
For their trip to the *co-operative.*

Queen Claude would be forgotten
Except for these small fruits:
Her years a bare two dozen,
Her back bent almost double,
She could never be as perfect as
These gold globes streaked with
green,
Misty like opals,
Luscious.

In the gloom of our summer
I think of your orchard
Where for a week we panned for
gold
In rivers of *Reine Claude* trees.

We picked nuggets big as walnuts
To place in the wooden boxes,
Our arms and mouths and bellies
So full,
      so full,
          so full.

Rosemary

The first time we stood in my garden,
You admired the rosemary:
Holding its hundred arms aloft
Rubbing shoulders with us, making a charmed circle.
You closed your eyes,
Bruised a stem in your hands, took a long breath,
And in the heart of summer I inhaled winter, incense,
All my Christmases.
Where rosemary flourishes, you said, the woman rules the house,
And somehow it thrives here under my neglect.
I am grateful for its permanence, glad of its power,
And though I need no ointment, salve or liniment,
I only have to reach my arm to find
A sprig for my pillow to ward off witches,

A tea for headaches, wine for gout, a purseful against plague,
An oil to mummify, a torch to purify,
A spear for friendship, remembrance, love.

My grandmother said rosemary never grew taller than Christ
Or older than his 33 years.
We have two decades yet before we know for sure.

Meanwhile it is rich and handsome
And we are rosemary spendthrifts,
Turning shoulders and legs of lamb into porcupines
With forests of fragrant spines,
Studding the roast pork,
Sprinkling the salads,
Spiking the summer potatoes,
Stirring it into Italian sauces.

In summer, when our daughter is asleep,
The garden calls us out.
We drink in the last of the light
And breathe the incense inching up the wall.
Brighter greens come and go, but always
It is dark green above, downy grey under,
And suddenly, a scatter of lilac stars.

Conor Farrell

Conor is a native of Dublin city. He has worked across a range of media. He has directed one film, *Inisheer – An Carraig Thiar* and produced and presented a weekly jazz music programme on Irish radio. Conor's press work includes a stint with *Honduras This Week*, an English language publication in that country and he is currently working on a film script and with his band The Prairie Dawgs who run the Tumbleweed Love Sessions at the Cobblestone Bar in Dublin 7. On September 12th 2001, Conor set out on a trip around the world. The following is an extract from his memoir of his adventures.

Oh My Buddha!

Michael's biting sarcasm somehow didn't match the contemplative glow of the embers or the hypnotic roar of the waterfall. As usual he had a lot to say but before long he had softened towards us and spoke rather intimately of a troubled past. He spoke bitterly of a broken relationship, a father he hadn't spoken to in years, a kind-hearted but sad mother, an estranged son he wanted a close relationship with and finally a painful heroin addiction. Michael's bitterness was palpable with just a mild dilution of weariness.

Before long the topic had shifted to that of the Golden Triangle where you could buy anything from precious stones to hard drugs. The Golden Triangle was the name given to the infamous opium-producing, mountainous area which covers the borders of Thailand, Burma, Laos & Vietnam. During World War II the Americans and the British had enlisted the help of the local tribes in this region against the Japanese and again against Communist Chinese at one point with promises of independent states Promises hadn't been kept and many mercenaries turned to illegal trading on the borders. Farangs had for many years been attracted to this area where they could purchase diamonds, rubies, emeralds, and scores of semi precious stones. Drug trade also flourished in the area and opium addiction had become a major problem amongst many tribesmen. Michael had visited the border and had been offered many such precious stones and more.

It probably shouldn't have come as a surprise when Michael finally produced a vial of white powder that he had procured at the Golden Triangle. However, the sight of it alone made us more than a little nervous. I felt that even looking at it could land us in a lot of trouble. Michael had constantly referred to his drug habit in the past tense. He was "over all of that now". But what was this? Surely someone of his intelligence knew that there is no such thing as a casual hit for an ex-junkie? He proceeded to tell us how he was going to fill a couple of film canisters with the powder and send it back to his home in Canberra. Yet I'm sure it was Michael, with his seemingly expansive knowledge of the Thai legal system, who told me of 3 young Australians who had recently been jailed for trafficking. The three 20-somethings, after much foreign diplomacy had seemingly escaped the standard death penalty and were given 50 years in a Bangkok prison – a fate worse than death, to my mind. Michael knew all of this and more but alas self-denial is the most deadly weapon of the subconscious. I urged Michael to put it away, looking nervously around me as if expecting to see a SWAT team descend dramatically from the trees above. It was getting late and although we kept talking for some time I was a little uneasy and was anxious to retire.

It must have been about 4 am when we stumbled back to our bamboo hut, having talked ourselves sober. Sleep came swiftly for us. That night I flew over the waterfall, across the tops of banana and coffee plantations, into the Karen village, over hills and rocks, and into slumber deep ...

Karla and I woke up the next morning to the sound of the waterfall and the golden rays of sunlight that streamed into our hut. I peeked outside only to be greeted by a grinning Michael. "Top o the mornin' to you Conor," he said in his best 'stage Oirish' accent. As my senses struggled one by one to reconstruct the world that morning had presented to me, I caught the smell of Joe's cooking. A cup of tea and some breakfast was the only answer! A bleary-eyed Eric expressed his amazement at the ability of the Irish to drink all night and appear bright the next morning. Bright??? Perhaps Eric had forgotten to put his lenses in that morning or was still a little drunk himself. At breakfast Joe briefed us on the day's itinerary — elephant rides, plenty more trekking & some white water rafting, so we needed an early start. It all sounded very exciting but a little bit too active to contemplate before breakfast. Looking for a short cut out of hell, I followed Stefan down to the waterfall for the last time before we went on our way.

****

Three nights later I awoke from a terrible dream. It was 4am. I immediately arose and walked into the bathroom. Soon all of Chaing Mai would be rising. Market stalls would be set up - skinny dogs would sniff around the canal banks, 'songthaews' and rickshaws would speed up and down outside our hotel, blasting their horns, looking for generous 'farangs' for fares. The sun would rise & Buddha would smile down upon this beautiful old Siamese city. I switched on the light above the mirror and stared back at my sleepy eyes. What was I dreaming of? Reluctant to go back to bed I splashed my face & stared more closely at my puzzled reflection searching for clues. I knew we would have to get up shortly. Our bus would be leaving this charming city for Bangkok later in the morning. From there we would fly to Australia after 9 weeks travelling in Asia. Where should we go for breakfast? I thought. It will be a long bus ride to Bangkok. "Bangkok", I said aloud, noting how strange it suddenly sounded. My thoughts drifted back to the 3 Australians imprisoned there for drug trafficking. I imagined how they must weep at night, begging God, Buddha or whomever to turn back the clock. "Were things that bad that we had to do such a foolish thing", I imagined them thinking over and over. For a brief moment I could feel their utter despair and felt anxious to leave, lest such a horrible fate should befall us.

But why would it? I thought about the previous night.

We had gone to dinner together – the entire group, with the exception of our guide Jungle Joe who had to start trekking with a new group at 6am. It was a beautiful night and such was our rapport that we were all genuinely sad saying our goodbyes. We exchanged e-mail addresses and invitations to our native lands. Libo even talked about setting up a forum where we could chat and exchange photos etc. (he never did, of course). Angelo, much to Laura's surprise, was quite drunk. The otherwise serious Dutch businessman, who usually remained reserved and very much in control, had loosened up and dared to enjoy himself. It was obvious from Laura's reaction that this was out of character for Angelo so she embraced the opportunity to let her hair down also. Sonya, who had planned to go to Australia, made arrangements to meet up with us in Sydney (which we did), and Eric invited us to stay with him in Los Angeles when we arrived there (which we didn't).

But even Joe had remarked on how well we bonded as a group. "Most of my groups can't wait to go their separate ways after spending a few days in the jungle together" he said. "but you are special, you make Jungle Joe's life so much easier". Then he went on to tell us about some troublesome groups he had in the past – a Japanese couple stopping every 5 minutes to take photographs of trees and rocks - an arrogant Swede who complained about everything from Joe's cooking right down to the fact that the group were expected to walk – an obese American student who simply couldn't keep up – and a very menstrual German girl who spent the whole weekend sobbing uncontrollably. It soon became clear to me that the necessary skills for Joe's job went far beyond the obvious, and it became even clearer why Joe liked our group so much. In that moment I believed that Joe meant it. In that moment I believed that we were an exceptional group and that Joe favoured us above all. In that moment I believed every dramatic twist and turn of his well rehearsed anecdotes.

Michael and Stefan lingered awhile with Karla and me that night after everyone else had gone. We were all going the same direction anyway and decided to go for one more beer before retiring. Karla and I were excited about our journey ahead — a brief stopover in Bangkok and on to Cairns, Australia. Michael too seemed more relaxed as if he had left something behind in the jungle — an old monkey perhaps, that had been on his back for far too long. He didn't speak as much but when he did he spoke more positively. He even tried to dissuade us from going to Sydney or Melbourne and offered to put us up for as long as we liked in his house in Canberra. Stefan on the other hand was far more chatty than usual. The Bavarian plumber too seemed very relaxed and happy. Michael showed us his journal, which everyone had signed earlier. The comments were all very warm and interesting. Libo, very frankly, had written that he didn't like Michael when he met him first but had seen quite a different side to him over the couple of days that we spent in the jungle, and now had much respect for him. But Stefan's very moving confessional was strangest of all. He empathized with Michael's addiction having gone through the same hell himself in back in Germany. He had lost years of his life to heroin before finally cleaning up and getting a trade.

When at last we finished our beer we decided to head back to our hotel and Stefan, who had moved to the same hotel as us, decided to go also. The night wasn't over yet for Michael. The last I saw of him he was getting a light from a local and asking about late bars. The typically friendly Thai gave Michael a big wide smile and pointed with his bony forefinger across the canal. Michael respectfully clasped his hands together, bowed his head and gave his thanks, "Kap Kun Krap", before disappearing into the crowd. I wondered if we would ever see him again.

Whatever foul dream had disturbed my sleep in the early hours of the morning was long gone. I was wide awake now, had showered and was starting to shave. It was still very early and Karla was sound asleep. I would be tired later but I knew that I could sleep on the bus to Bangkok. Bangkok! The torment of the three young Australians returned to me. I thought of how uncomfortably close we had been to a little vial of white powder — and how looking at it could damn us to the same fate as the Adelaide Three. What had Michael done with it anyway? It was more than he could consume over a few days, he told us. Was he really going to post it to his address? How else could he get it home? Taking it through the airport would be insane. Unless....? Suddenly I was gripped with fear. How many stories had I heard about innocent travellers being set up.

Surely he wouldn't....but I couldn't get the thought out of my mind. I had grown very fond of Michael but how far can you trust someone who is bound to heroin. He said he was an ex-junkie, but I had seen the blatant contradiction right before my eyes. Couldn't the most noble person with junk in their veins sell their own mother for a hit? And who are we to Michael anyway. Perhaps I was being ridiculous. Maybe I was just paranoid! I walked out of the en-suite bathroom and gazed at Karla. She was in a deep sleep. For a brief moment all was silent but for her gentle breathing. Then suddenly a distant bark, then the beeping of a lone cab driver a few blocks away. I felt a trickle down my neck. I put my hand to my neck. Blood! I glanced at the razor in my hand. Damn-it, how careless of me. Now I could hear the distant voices, which seemed to echo on the street. Dawn comes early in Chang Mai. How beautiful for the free and yet surely a cruel mockery from the heavens for the incarcerated.

About halfway along the road from Chang Mai to Bangkok, I managed to get a seat. Karla had a seat for most of the journey but was squashed between suitcases & rucksacks & an uncharacteristically large Thai guy. I had little sleep the night before and was so happy & relieved to finally get a seat. I laughed at how frantic I had been that morning. I must have looked the epitome of good sense and reason with blood stained shaving foam on one side of my face, while emptying all our bags in the hope that unwanted little packages weren't taking refuge therein. I thought of Joe and his new group of trekkers. I think it only occurred to me then that this was his job and his life – another day, another dollar. I wondered if he was telling the same awful jokes and the same stories. I imagined he was, and suddenly a very warm feeling came over me and in that instant I felt a love for Jungle Joe.

And what about our fellow trekkers? I wondered where they were that morning. Had Angelo returned to his old serious demeanour? I imagined Laura sitting with him over breakfast in silence while he squinted at the newspaper in denial of his hangover. Perhaps in another hotel across town Libo spared no technical details enthusing to a patient Lillian about how his 'hill trekkers' website would be no ordinary one! Elsewhere, I imagined Eric whispering sweet nothings to Sonya. Sweet nothings and alas ill-fated promises. While in the same hotel on the next floor, a reborn Stefan sang loudly in the shower as he contemplated his next destination. But most of all, I wondered about Michael? In my mind's eye I could place him anywhere. Reading a newspaper at a canal side café. Maybe complaining about the Thais' crazy driving to some random backpacker trying desperately to remain unnoticed. Or, perhaps, he was haggling with some tuk tuk driver or down at the market. Or anywhere really! Anywhere with a cigarette in one hand and a beer in the other.

I looked back at Karla. She had miraculously managed to fall sleep as the bus hopped up and down. Would Chang Mai be one of the highlights of our travels? I knew we had another year to go – Australia , New Zealand, Honduras! I felt euphoric. *Oh My Buddha!*

Shane Harrison

Shane Harrison was born in Dublin. He graduated from the National College of Art and Design in the early '80s and has worked in television, advertising and as a freelance designer. His first collection of short stories, *Blues Before Dawn,* was published by Poolbeg in 1992 and his collection *The Benefits of Tobacco* was published by 40 Foot Press. He has also contributed stories, articles and reviews to a range of newspapers and periodicals. He has a BA degree in English literature from Dublin City University and currently works as a librarian in County Wicklow. The following story was written by Shane.

The Aeroplane Trap.

Gabriel had a flame for one of the German students. It was not like him. Despite his easy way with women he was essentially of the type that would naturally be referred to as a bachelor - interest but no infatuation, intent but without purpose. With Petra I could see the attraction. She came in most days, sometimes to read, sometimes to surf the net, but at all times a contained tempest of suntan and silvery detachment. She was, as were most of the best and brightest, taken under Gabriel's golden wing but his charm was slightly blunted in Petra's case by the persistent weakness of her English. Meanwhile his ardour was further stoked by her silence.

As the flame burnt ever brighter, Gabriel developed the notion that I was fluent, or at least conversant, in German. I came to represent to him the key to unlocking Petra's stony citadel.

I have no idea how I happened to impart such an impression. Perhaps Gabriel was impressed by my frequent flying hours in a lifetime of package and backpack holidays. He was a homebird, a necessary condition given his dislike for modern modes of transport, his fear of flying. Yet the fact remained that my linguistic powers were almost entirely confined to English - my Irish was poor, my French lousy, my German non-existent!

Perhaps not entirely non-existent.

As a residue of those backpacking days, in the forced camaraderie of Europe's hostels - filed away there amongst the blurred friendships, one night stands and delirium tremens, there is a sentence:

In meiner freizeit ich mache gern model flugzeuge.

I happily gave this to Gabriel as a bauble with which he might impress the fraulein. He easily committed it to memory and took some supplementary advice on delivery. Make eye contact and maintain it, I advised.

"In meiner freizeit ich mache gern model flugzeuge." Gabriel pauses. "I trust it's not something rude or gross."

"Not at all," I assured him.

"It wouldn't give offence?"

Even in these politically correct times, I could not see how it would give offence.

The next day I was in the History section for rather a long time. I was correlating the French Revolution and Romantic poetry. Bliss was it in that dawn to be alive, I read; perhaps with appropriate prescience as I spied Gabriel striding down the aisle towards me.

"You cunt," he said, amiably.

"But to be young was very heaven," I continued, aloud, then asked him how he had got on with Petra.

"She thinks I'm an anorak!"

"But you are an anorak."

   Gabriel paused only briefly. "Model aeroplanes, for fuck sake!" It was unlike him to curse. "What can she think of me now?"

It was true, I suppose. Petra's attitude had subtly changed, loosened even. But the smirk that played on those subtle lips was not the smile of invitation. She was greatly amused, fondly amused, but alas nothing more.

   "Model aeroplanes." Gabriel sighed.

   "But only in your spare time. Don't you see? Don't you find it...enigmatic?"

   "I don't recognise spare time, you bollix." (Okay, he knew some regular swear words.) Gabriel stuck out his chin, aggressively. "And what do you do in your spare time?"

And what do you do in your spare time?

In truth, much of that was taking up with smoking and drinking. There was also thinking, thinking being alternatively devoted to, these days, Aristotle's Poetics and their relevance to modern theatre and Isabella's body. I don't here disavow Isabella's mind, wondrous fascinating and deeply engaged on most of our meetings, but not thought about in absentia with the same desire as I thought about her body.

I lay with Isabella on a silver strand. She said she liked to paint the Great Bear on the chest of her lovers. White pinpricks against the dark skin. Ursa Minor too, Orion if the fancy took her.

   "It is a hobby of mine and I can be both angel and slut." She has to explain. "As an angel I fly among the stars. As a slut I've been fucked by the northern hemisphere."

   I was enchanted. Here was a symmetry between love and aesthetics which I had not suspected. Yet, for all that there was the question of the words used. The right words. "And what does the true lover say?" I asked.

   "There are so many, Europe is a big country."

   "Just one line then, one line from the perfect lover."

   She bent over my shoulder. In the cusp of silence, between the thumping of the surf, she whispered in my ear. In my pink shell...

Ross Hattaway

Ross Hattaway was born in New Zealand and has lived in Ireland since 1990. He has published poetry in periodicals and collections, including *Writings* (Wellington), *Life Beyond the Louvres* (Northern Territory Anthology), *Poetry Australia*. His readings include the Poetry Ireland Introduction Series, Anna Livia FM, Between the Lines (Belfast), Chapter and Verse, the Last Wednesday Series, Ó Bhéal and The White H ouse Poets. His first collection of poetry *The Gentle Art of Rotting* was published by Seven Towers in 2006. In 2008 Ross was a guest at the Poetry Spring Festival in Lithuania, becoming the first Irish poet to guest at that festival. Part of The Gentle Art of Rotting was translated into Lithuanian and published as part of the festival celebration. Also in 2008, Ross was a guest of the Live Poet's Society in Sydney. The following poem and short extract are by Ross.

The New Cooking

Ready, Steady, Fornicate.
Can't Fornicate, Won't Fornicate.
Fornicating with Nigella.
Fornicating, not wishing to discriminate, with Rhodes.
The F word.
Ramsay's Bedroom Nightmares.
The Galloping Gourmet
Fornicator.
Fornicate with Fanny,
although not in colour.
Two Fat Ladies (on a motorbike)
Fornicating.
School Dinners with... no,
maybe not.
French Fornicating Made Simple.
Fornicating for Beginners.
The Ten Minute Fornicator.
Fornicating for Health.
Fornicating for Life.
The Organic Fornicator.
Vegetarian Fornicating at Home
You are What You Fornicate.
And, for the young leaving home
in these straitened times,
Fornicating for Flatters and
Fornicating on a Budget.

Fornicating – a hobby for life.
The new cooking.

Extract:

The Afters, **From** *Cutting Down Trees*

The band was on a break but the afters guests had hit the bar and were catching up with the main bunch. All you could do was sit back and watch.

At the back of the room, Uncle Lex was arguing with a waiter, who looked relieved at not having to go back to the widows' table. Over at the stage, Aunty Collie was swaying by herself, even though there wasn't any music. She stopped, leaned over and gently vomited into the open mouth of a saxophone. No one seemed to notice. She went back to trying to light a cigarette.

The reason no one noticed Aunty Collie vomiting into the saxophone was that the bridesmaids were stripped to the waist and slugging it out in front to the stage – a dispute, it emerged later, over who ordered a round of crème de menthe bomb shells and therefore who should pay for them. As the band returned, the matron of honour decked the groom's sister with a fine left hook when she tried to break it up. The band gave her a drum roll. It was a very good punch.

As the groom's other sisters tried to stem the blood and the matron of honour wailed about breaking her hand, I was distracted by the sight of Johnny G, neighbour and a compact 120 kilos of social drinker, staggering towards me, with some sort of bag hanging out of his shirt. He collapsed into a chair beside me, muttering about escaping from the youngest grandson, who was being used by the others, in the relentless pursuit of sugary drinks and salty snacks, as the impact whinger. He unbuttoned the shirt, took the bag out, put it on the table and drained his beer.

Jesus, that's a relief, he said, So unfuckincomfortable. 'Sokay, Ron, I'll move it in a mo, jus' lemme get my breath.

At first, I could only stare. Then I moved my pint. It appeared to be a colostomy bag.

This is going to be a big night, Johnny.

And, he said, it's only just begun.

R. Nemo Hill

R. Nemo Hill was born in Massapequa, Long Island. Blithely eschewing academics as a youth, he chose instead for a teacher the contingencies of travelling with a bag full of books and a few cotton tee-shirts. A small solitary stone house on the coast of Portugal proved quite educational in this regard. Returning to New York in the mid-eighties he had various free verse poems published in such journals as *Sulfur, Mid-American Review, Multiples,* and *Blue Light Review.* He has since then been travelling frequently to Southeast Asia, especially Indonesia, and more recently Thailand and Myanmar. In 2002 he published, in collaboration with painter Jeanne Hedstrom, an illustrated novel *(Pilgrim's Feather, Quantuck Lane Press).* 2004 saw the publication of a book-length poem, based upon a short story by H. P. Lovecraft *(The Strange Music of Erich Zann, Hippocampus Press).* His most recent work has appeared in *Iambs & Trochees, Smartish Place, Shit Creek ReviewS* and *Ambit (UK).* His chapbook *Prolegomena To An Essay On Satire* was published by Modern Metrics Press 2006. Experiments with satirical verse forms include a 2300-line epic based loosely upon Alexander Pope's Rape of the Lock *(A Gumbo Abandoned)* as well as a somewhat graphic conversation with the Lord Byron of Don Juan *(The Long View).* Both these long poems will be published in by Seven Towers in Winter 2009/2010. The following poem is by Nemo.

Murmuring Firmament, Wandering Fundament

[This poem freely alludes to the work of St.-John Perse, T. S. Eliot, Samuel Beckett, the tiny notebooks of William Rice, the comedy of Scotty The Blue Bunny, and young Moss's waking dream.]

1

Cold water underneath the bridge surrounds me.
Save for one weedy pylon, slick with slime,
that water would undoubtedly have drowned me.
I buck the current current — stopping time.
A bitter barnacle I cling —
                                befoamed,
awash in memories not wholly mine,
caught in the fundamental flow below —
life's flotsam and its jetsam and its then some
merged into one vast mumbling undertow.

I'm bathed, I'm buffeted —
                                by scurf, by scum,
by cast-off refuse, by the swelling stream
of exiled moments, moments said and done.
Exposed half to the air, half sub-marine,
must all discarded, orphaned moments float
and bloat like corpses? Waterlogged, obscene,
seaward they pass — a fleet of stinking boats.
A wrack rejected. Raft of weed and waste.
A stain upon vast waters. Banished ghosts.

Choked by familiar flux, it's I alone that's braced
(like paper in a wind on fence-wire snagged)
against the tide that laps this bridge's base.
And not until the bridge itself be dragged
from its Titanic legs of pillared stone
shall I, last castaway, lose anchorage
and be at last swept downstream, out to sea,
and lost far from all human memory.

2

Eyes stinging and back-blinking murky water
and clearing to catch one more fleeting glimpse,
one more still photograph of calm, arched stone:
the belly of the bridge of crossing, crossing

far overhead in pregnant shadow, while
marooned in my loose layer of cold lava

eye lay listening.
How did I get here?
"We were waiting with our horses by the borders of the bay."
Upon what perch these beasts of futile memory, foreign,
feeding?
Shall I then let go of this wet stone?
Or linger on, look up, and listen to
all that which once upon a time was true
and now's un-inter-locking, lacking all
significance?
"Turn over with your stylus,
on the table of the shores, O Scribe,
Oh Scribe
the wax impressed with the empty statement."

Still holding on like weary Atlas, rooted in
the shadow of the bridge's vault above me —
deep in the belly of the bridge of crossing
I hear the echoes of the steps and wheels,
the wagons and the carts delivering goods —
eggs, cheese, marbles, chips, chops, and dominoes,
cheap socks for the kids, rolls of quarters,
fine days and foul days, the rain and the shine,
and the battered flasks of spirits.
Horse. Cow. Donkey. Dog. Cat.
Lost child. Bad man. Blue bird. New car. Old hat.
Traffic.
"Ah! Let them burn,
let them burn on the sand-capes,
all this refuse of feather, fingernail, dyed hair, impure linen" and
the drops of rainwater
hanging from the ear-lobes of the Buddha in the plaster garden and
the fat unpleasant man in his car listening to an unbearably passionate
aria on cassette tape and
the groceries fallen from the bag, torn or tipped, and
flattened by the tires of passing cars and
a penny with two heads or two tails and

"Princess Diana who was so sweet retarded people used to lick her face".
What if all the sadness surfaced in one season,
a single day or hour, one sodden second —

the infant's, the mid-life-like and the old,
the mammal-cry, the plant's tear — all told?

Perhaps I slipped from stool to floor, lay flat, and said,
"My god, here's what cannot be known — I'm dead."
Perhaps I lay now in a pool of adversarial liquids
which do not mix, but like an oil and
water (bright red oil and dirty water)
rise now the one and now the other to
a swift receding surface.
                          Or did I leap?
like some disheartened bridegroom half my age,
to expiate lost love or other heinous crimes?
Did I topple like a drunken adolescent?
Stumble like an elderly sleepwalker?
Dive like a gambler at great loss, sink like a stone,
drop like a victim of the latest pox, or melt
O Scribe,
                 ". . . *Like one who strips at sight of the sea*" ?
Did I splashdown dauntless like an astronaut?
Or did I merely lose my fragile foolish footing
or slit my wrists and faint and fall forgetting?
Still farther yet
above or yet below
past mumbling mid-realms dare I go —?
Thunder and lightning and solar dusts and
titanic rumblings' crust —.
Through violent nature's vacuum
young Tom Eliot's last 3 calls
Jove's jagged bolt
Van Winkle's solemn nine-pins
God's empty rolling barrels or new noisy upstairs neighbors
or great Raja-Naga's indigestion in the treasured depths.
Lost in the thought I brood
without the fortitude
to act.

In a dream there *are* birds that live an inch and then are stung no more.

"Ya gotta have a woman and an idea...yes?"
Did the light change so I could cross the street, the bridge —
and make good my escape from what this old drunk sent
and from what the Thundering Murmur meant?

When the light changes
and the glittering on the sea becomes less blinding.
"(The shadow of a great bird falls on my face.)"
and I paraphrase the Saint Perseian women who straddle and lift
their flowering polyester skirts of Asia
to make water of K-Mart
on the banks of the great river.

So much water under the bridge.

3.

A thrum resounds, perhaps wet beat, or slosh,
perhaps a shissh of mere near collishion,
at most at times a hollowed heave-ho in of howls,
a splash of consonants bewhelmed
by single fundamental vowels.
The water underneath the bridge can't hold
the words which are, above, the casual coin —
— stern dialectic — the me-you-yes-no-bought-sold
of the realm of the commerce of crossing.
In the water under the bridge
such structures seldom can be found.
There—words soon dismantle themselves
in great waves of diminishing sound,
undone, unstitched, attuned to
a far scar of slower tone, of lower pitch.
For hours and days sometimes, head down,
I hear not any, no, not any, no, no human sound.
And then when with no warnings the wind to breath be-shifts, what's up rains
        down,
and it is in dismembered words I find I drown.
Confetti-like, I'm sprinkled with unpunctuable clause.
Jibs and tops and mainsheets severed from their splintered masts
sweep past the shipwrecked mariner.
By sirens still assailed,
stilled sailor, I can neither rise nor sink
but choke back the polluted water
and try vainly not to think.
Oh, but how they tug and purl in the basin of the brain!
These flags without poles!

Parts without wholes! Tell me,
O Scribe —
tell me the stories of old
that are the re-measurance of distance.

"He's really a mummy

and he's got a tattoo on his back. And when the sun goes down
he dies, and when it comes up he never comes back again."

he tells me, he tells me not
he tells me, he tells me not
he tells me, he tells me not

"And he waits until he turns into snow."

"You mean he has a lot of arms?"

not so

4.

When with no warning winds
all breath descends —
what's up and distant
rains close down,
each particle of lost confetti swoons with its own sound—
its own phonetic phantom, its own lost pronoun.
I repeat myself, of course,
but by the chatter of more than my own thoughts distressed
I find myself emblathered, babbled, and oppressed
by words of strangely equal force and weight
whose aching echoes do not dissipate
despite the tetherlessness of my fallen state.
   "But in fact he was not accurate when he claimed to have stopped working from
      the model."
   "Yeah, but now I have a new dilemma to deal with . . ."
   "How much was known in town about their battle?"
   "Everything you see is what nobody looks at."
   "And after all these days I can't change my ways."
   "We can talk to no one but ourselves about that."
   "Why is that fabulous worm always turned in the wrong direction?"
   "We've lasted long enough to finally share our illusions."
   "So I try and try again and again."

"Even though he's just someone to say good-bye to?"

With sheets of tracing paper [approx. 11 x 14 / 35.5 x 43 cm.]
I realized that I had arranged the leaves of all autumn
over the already painted figure.
Everything in its place.
But all far too far away.

Where all other characteristics of the storm are only intermittently present,
the bottom nature is constant—
but only in the sense of constantly repeating itself.
Its fundamental character is only registered in time's holocaustic dream
repeatedly present
precisely wandering
through every act & condition & event of human being.

                                        "Attention!
Please wait for our very respectful landing officer to assist you
in your descent!" *"So when did he start dating his work so seriously?"*
Because that's not quite what I meant by descent.

"And so he becomes the Student of Dissolution?
Becomes old Jonah? Becomes the Fish . . . ?" *Well, yes,*
black was *frowned on by the academy of the time. I was taught*
that it was not *a color—that it should* not *be mixed—"* but
when what's up rains down it's *not* about showing one thing at a time
or else I wouldn't bother with the rhyme.
While the first is working his high-eye-art in his garden under a transparent
        pseudonym
the second works as fast as he can plagiarizing verses that more often than
        not
in fact very often I would say do *not* scan.
"Is that where the 2,000 francs went that summer?"
Is that how you paint a smell without any warning
when the wind becomes breath up-ended
and alters "the accent of the rose by changing its orientation," by inserting,
dragging to hard drive, clicking on eye, curving, rubber stamping,
choosing rush, pressing option, rubber band, and control panel?
There is a butterfly on the ladder in the library!
"And we have a great time
or so it seems
but the same thing
happens often in dreams."
But how—how can one travel to a place that one includes?

"I guess I have to keep explaining until it registers."

"You can't store much information in those little booklets."
"They work their asses off all covered with grease."
"He has 20 minutes."
"So close your eyes and train them on the floor."

Collaborate with me on one of my texts
and thereby rewrite our history.
"We might be a combination dynamic . . ."

"All of this reinforces my opinion that the process of transferring cartoons onto the
 large canvas
figured largely in the final resultlessness."

And now there are direct parallels:

"Need it and be fine."
"To be and claim it."
"The time that it is."
"Mount it up."
"Could they grow and tell it so?"
"He asked about it."
"They will say it is beautiful."
"Completely in measuring it."
"Letting it be left to me."

5.

Then all goes still
with the sudden silence of the uprooted.
Wind shifts, breath dies,
and lexis lies battered
(long roots and mud-caked tongues in tatters)
alongside that hole in the earth from which
it has been lately torn, its own grave —
that hole which quickly fills with water
here under the bridge of the dream of the crossing, where
no voice disturbs with quarreling tone
this watery expanse where I now float alone —
no voice, that is, except, of course, my own.

Sometimes a shadow falls from up above, one hurrying figure, Murphy,
maybe two, Molloy, Malone, or three, or four or ten, perhaps ten thousand,
    nameless —
each hurtling by on his errand, his desire, epic, trivial,
pragmatic, blind, inspired.
Truck stops. Melons are unloaded.
Glass cracks. Bullets are exploded.
Man weeps. Penis is inserted.
Sky falls. Atoms are converted.
Die's cast. Clothing's washed and folded.
Rope's tied. Wicked child is scolded.
Salad's tossed. Diary is entered.
Music plays. Photo's cropped and centered.
Dinner's cooked. Violent crime's committed
Keys turn. Fragrance is emitted.
Girl smiles. Counterfeit is tendered.
Stars cross. Weapons are surrendered
Water boils. Honor is defended
Time flies. Bed-time story's ended.
But all without a word this time,
in shadow-play, in pantomime,
in silent cinema-light, flickering in nervous agitation,
like crude home-movies that once upon a time were taken
while revisiting The Wasteland on a family vacation.
And you were there, and you were there, and you, and you —
and somehow, somehow we all seemed to muddle through
despite lost tickets, long cherished plans forsaken,
missed connections, misinterpreted directions,
a wicked case of dysentery that left us pale and shaken,
and those fleeting landscapes that left our hearts so close to breaking
and permanently scarred by all the roads not taken.

It seems so long ago. I had a fruit stall at the side of the road.
Everyone stopped there to buy things with pits and seeds and juice,
coins jingled, cars screeched to a halt brake linings whining.
"Thief! Thief!" cried an old woman, it began to snow, silver and white,
the moon rose, promises were made, a hole in my shoe, a hole in the carpet,
a tear in the fabric, fresh berries for sale,
don't ever leave me, don't think about it, don't say that,
fresh berries for sale, fresh berries berries berries for sale.
Is this what it means to have a past, my ancient or exhausted heart

delivered like a infant
by a strange ungainly bird, an albatrossian stork —
its living bleeding parcel swaddled in the cries of gulls
and the lapping of shallow waters against the empty shores of exile?
And the Angel of Annunciation appears, after the fact,
yawning mightily after a long journey —
blue wings, red tunic, hem torn, bag of groceries,
no batteries, no particular quality to the light in his grey eyes,
he's got the whole world in his hands
and his copper trumpet is blowing bass bubbles underwater.
"I come to announce what has already departed!"
"We were waiting for you
with our horses
by the borders of the bay . . ."
O Scribe! Record for me the echoes of a former day.

6.

What is it that I'm trying so hard to say?

Why do I find myself so far away
from all I once deemed nearest — mine — my own?
The water underneath the bridge flows on

and wears all flesh away, down to the bone;
and were it not for language and its grip
from this slight mooring I would surely slip

and sink like any other wounded ship
beneath the waves of all that come and go —.
Yet these brief fleeting moments can bestow

a word — that word I'd rescue from the foam —
that message in a bottle, word submerged,
that yet can break the surface on the verge

of its oblivion — unsepulchred,
it rises up exhausted from mute time
and through a secret alchemy of rhyme

becomes the cradle and the grave and shrine

of all the sadness of what slips away from under
the given ground upon which all souls wander.

Far, far away, I hear a distant thunder.
The ever fugitive, elusive word,
the ruined word, unspoken, overheard,

the pole star of the ancient mariner,
the murmur of the ever-dying swan,
the deep reflection of the known unknown.

The only word, O Scribe, that I can call my own
as water underneath the bridge flows on and on.

Eileen Keane

Eileen's first short story won the Cecil Day Lewis fiction prize in 2004 and in 2007 her short story *Tryst* was one of 14 chosen through a competition on Seoige and O'Shea on RTE for an anthology called *Do the Write Thing* published by Poolbeg Press in aid of breast cancer research. Also in 2007 she won first prize in the humorous essay competition at Listowel. She is a visual artist and founder member of the Leinster Printmaking Studio in Clane, Co Kildare. She is also a member of the Clane writers group and has just completed her first novel. The following story is by Eileen.

The Cave

I'm not a fan of caves but when my kids wanted to go and see the Ailwee caves I agreed to the trip when they told me how educational it would be. I told them I'd been before and that I'd be happy to look around the Interpretative Centre and read about it over warm tea and a comforting scone while my husband brought them into the bowels of the earth.

The truth is I am afraid of being down under the ground in an enclosed space like a cave. Perhaps afraid is too strong a word, its more like a sense of unease, a feeling of the suspended earth overhead, its weight and mass. A sense of the fragility of the human body, of the delicacy of the veins and bloody runways of arteries racing along my highways. You might think my actions are totally selfish then since I am willing to allow those closest to me to go 'into the lion's den' as it were, but it's not that. I am aware of the ridiculousness of my irrational fears so I do not foist them on my family.

As I sip my tea in the café while I wait for their return I wonder if maybe there's something there in my genetic history that has programmed me to be wary. Some macho caveman that shut me up in a cave until I agreed to have his dinner on the table every evening at six o clock, or should I say, to have his bloody hunk of meat skinned and roasted and on the slab at sundown.

Maybe he didn't like the way I eyed up the hunter gatherers and waved my furry bits at them as I collected the berries for his wine. Or maybe he noticed the gamey look in my eye when I saw his friends helping to carry the bloody boar to our fire.

They might have been hairier, less advanced than him, but then I've always been turned on by excess body hair and sometimes brains just complicate things.

So he makes me stay in the cave when he has friends around and when I cry and won't rut with him, he relents a bit, and moves a rock in the cave wall so there's an opening like a letter box, and he lets me sit there in the evenings and watch them as they drink and have wrestling matches.

But then he has no-one to stoke up the fire and bring more food, so after a while he gets the idea of sewing some skins together into a kind of tent that he puts over my head and he cuts out a space for my eyes, and then he is happy because even if I have a gamey look in my eyes the lads don't really see me any more and I have to retreat into my head and think up bitchy thoughts to throw at the other women down at the stream in the morning.

I'm stirring my tea and laughing to myself at what a crazy kind of mind I have when a man asks to share my table. He stares at me in what I think is a disapproving manner and I feel unreasonably guilty and anxious as I make my way to the exit of the cave. When my husband Tommy comes out with the kids safe and sound.

I throw my arms around him and hug him hard and tell him its his turn to make dinner this evening.

Noel King

Noel King was born in Tralee, Co Kerry, where he still lives and where he runs Doghouse Books. A prizewinner in the William Allingham Short Story Competition, his poetry collection *Counterparts*, is in preparation. The following two poems are by Noel.

The Third Attempt

At dinner she'd pressed
a delicate fork in
moving the fish-flesh
from the bones,
then played a while
with it on the edge
of her plate.
No one noticed.

Then she made up real special,
wore the new Christmas dress,
held the boyfriend's hand
going out the door.

The family dog screamed
in the night; they found
her feet first
in the shed
after the disco.

Watercolour Christmas

It was almost Christmas Eve
When you went to pluck holly, cut the tree.
I, the last child, waited, frustrated
impatient to decorate the house as you
and your forefathers had done.

Holly was barren that year.
It frightened you, a sign of things,
you said you'd never seen it without berries.
I asked why the trees were so quiet this year,
And what holly stood for.
It's an old custom, you said.
It hit me that, although aged, you didn't know everything.

I placed it to hide high spots
where faded biscuit tins with fishing gear emerged
and cardboard boxes kept batteries,
cartridges warm until Spring.

I took tiny beads, dunked my fingers
in watercolour red, dried them on newspaper
under my bed; glued them on holly branches.
Look Granny, look, we found some with berries.
Visitors admired my holly too,
marvelled at how we'd found it.
That Christmas night one bead popped
to the floor, then another and another.
I, red-faced said: sure aren't all decorations false nowadays.
They all just laughed.

Quincy R Lehr

Quincy is a native of Oklahoma, recently returned to New York City after an extended stint living in Ireland. His work has appeared in numerous journals internationally, including *The Barefoot Muse, Cadenza, Crannog, The Dark Horse, Decanto, Iambs & Trochees, The Raintown Review,* and *The Shit Creek Review.* His first full-length collection, *Across the Grid of Streets,* was published by Seven Towers earlier this year. Quincy is Associate Editor of *The Raintown Review.* The following poem is by Quincy.

TRIPTYCH

Saturday Morning

The driving scourge, the contour of the flesh
that, flayed past any wisdom, turns to mush,
the sudden surge of wounds exposed afresh;
they lead to ruptures. As the fissures gush,

Bathsheba's bastards from the illicit tumble
will stare at shadows, too fucked-up and frightened
to keep their act together. They let things crumble
and leave the kingdom weakened, unenlightened.

His clothing crumpled by the mantelpiece
seems to rustle slightly with his snore
that echoes with a vacuous release.
Though no one's there, she glances at the door.

And now she turns to stare at the pictures on
the mantel, disarrayed by last night's passion,
disturbed or just knocked over as the dawn
approached — but a progression in a fashion.

A dark-haired little girl, with all the schmaltz
of knee-length dresses, ponytails, and dolls,
a gap-toothed smile that doesn't (yet) seem false...
or maybe a tomboy dressed in overalls

with Tonka truck in hand. A ballerina?
A Daddy's Girl? A miniature of Mom?
A gymnast aiming for the sports arena?
A future heartbreak waiting for her prom?

A picture's static image can't reveal
the uncommemorated days — nor can it
capture in light the way she used to feel
some day beneath the sun on this blue planet.

The past is breached; the front collapses in.
She grasps his hand, a gesture faked by rote,
rehearsed in daydreams, wheedled out with gin.
A rumbling noise comes belching from his throat.

The neighbours note the unfamiliar car
and wonder how their property will smell
when downwind from the backwash of the bar.
His car's up on the kerb, parked parallel.

The burglar of the body shifts and farts.
He gets up, staggers off, and urinates.
She groans, and her defences come apart
like shredded cocktail napkins, but she waits

for him to come to bed to throw him out.
Shock ricochets across his face. He rises,
dresses, holding back a furious shout
against the 'fucking bitch'. He leaves. The crisis

is done for now, until another night,
another business trip that leaves her stranded,
lonely, and bored, with ravenous appetite
for some companionship, cajoled, demanded—

with the same results. Convenient fictions,
raw material for the shrink next week —
catharsis, yes, but mixed with dark predictions
of too much booze, a passable physique.

It does no good when he has gone away
to say it didn't happen. Nonetheless,
she sets those thoughts aside, and through the day,
the light streams in; she watches motionless.

And where the hell's Uriah as she moans
another's name (or was it his?) in bed —
'off on business'? Even though he phones —
she knows his mind is somewhere else instead,

perhaps his job and keeping her in style
while keeping far away to play at power
in conference rooms. She'll bear it for a while,
but waits for David to see her in the shower.

Saturday Afternoon

The chic cafe in the poshest shopping centre,
a caramel macchiato and a paper,
while strains of some obese Italian tenor
stir in the background. But his arias taper

into some singer with a soft guitar.
The CD's at the counter, and her friends
shift the conversation to the star
they barely hear. The tangent hits its end,

then on to the news and gossip and the kids
that Katie hasn't had, persistent rumours
that she'd hit — and here I quote — 'the skids'.
Innuendoes metastasise like tumours.

The sagging eyelids give it all away,
the fumble for her purse, the murmured hex
against the brightness of this Saturday
afternoon. A subtle stench of sex

clings to her body like cologne. She shifts
self-consciously beneath their judging gazes,
narrowed with knowing, and by the time she lifts
the coffee to her lips, the staring blazes.

'Are you coming to the benefit?'
Yeah right. They have to ask. Recall the scene
last winter? Then they're talking baby shit,
God knows what else. How to keep things clean

without the hired help. And what was that?
Yes, it's Dior, and yes it's new. I know
you only mean to say I'm getting fat.
But you can't say these things out loud. God, no.

The etiquette of malice is quite subtle,
especially served cold, reduced to craft,
shrewd as diplomacy. Emotions scuttle
the delicate interplay upon a raft

of those who tolerate each other. School
or charities or work; it doesn't matter.
Each has its own, unstated Golden Rule.
'Do unto others...'? Bullshit! Stick to chatter,

never show weakness. Don't come out and say it,
insinuate. And never show your hand
but damn well know how you intend to play it,
aggressive and ruthless, eager for command.

Sunday Evening

And there she is, a model for us all,
brunette and buxom, eyes widely set and blue,
wasp waist, long legs, ever so slightly tall,
the stuff of songs. And what's a man to do

except applaud? This woman's our ideal,
a huge collective hard-on, and we see her
emerge from the contestants, almost real,
as also-rans exhale and want to be her...

drunk and spoken for and slightly mad,
a strapless gown but frumpy underwear,
weeping as the scene turns mopey-sad —
tragic or pathetic, do we care?

Well, not tonight. The moral is the same
as it is every night, at home or out,
alone or with another. Sobs of shame
from well-known sources follow every bout

till she collapses, sick, unsatiated,
into a pillow with a lusty snore.
Turn out the lights, angry but sedated.
Head for the couch and softly close the door.

The nights are cold despite the thermostat,
the duvet that she wraps up around her feet.
The nights are always dark despite the flat
outside glimmers — pale, devoid of heat.

'It's hard being beautiful'; the expectations
prove too much sometimes, and so she rests
swathed in blankets against these situations,
arms crossed defensively beneath her breasts

against intruders, husbands, and such lovers
as come her way. It's much more cosy here
behind the door and underneath the covers.
Repeat, repeat. There goes another year.

A few more hairs turn grey; a few more lines
crinkle from her eyes; a bit more sag
lowers her bosom. An old dress underlines
a thin expanse of flab. But still, she'll brag

about the pictures on the mantelpiece,
a woman she resembles, but never was.
She'll pay a shrink to rant to for 'release',
trying to figure out the things that cause

her to be like this, but in the night,
there's just recrimination as the drink
recedes, and fears of age and cellulite
take over. *Screw it. Tell it to your shrink*

if you'll feel better, but I'm through with you,
your false 'new starts'. That tragic diva pose,
the things you weep — even when they're true.
Hangovers wait beneath the pile of clothes.

Colm Lundberg

Colm Lundberg is a writer from Dublin currently hiding in Kerry. He is currently posing as a civil servant while also pretending to be a writer, poet and playwright, but he hopes to get better soon. He has written several children's books by accident on the topic of mental illness which he hopes will be published soon. To quote a local newspaper in which he was recently interviewed, "Colm is also a dog owner". The following two poems are by Colm.

Dayglo™ Twenty-One

At dew-entangled cross-roads
A one pathed Polykleitos beckons,
And the poet assumes the reader knows who Polykleitos is.
The Tuesday-sour coffee mornings
Fill a rich aroma of iconoclast conformity.
The I, the you — a Barbie doll —
In my day it was different;
I was for sale a different mercenary.

The Dayglo™ Twenty-One of us
Pick a peppered pigeonhole,
And like a statue the pigeon shit
Rests on heads — theirs or ours.
They.

Copyright a soul! It's patent 01,
God has the rights — a legality!
Impermissible evidence, your honour
God has not responded to her subpoena.

Smoke a joint, the yellow wood
Dayglo ™ Twenty-One Mark II.
Your obsolete, a Pentium block in microcosmic universe.
Delve among the dirty socks and pocket fluff
To pick the scabs off dead skin.

Dayglo™ Twenty-One still needs batteries.
They're not included, you know.

Relocation

It's all the same old bullshit, y'know.
Bigger place, more people, same humanity
Or lack thereof.
Names of pubs, clubs and tourist traps
Have been changed to infect the innocent.
The only thing to do is get rich —
Then you can have your any vice, no matter where you live.

People still have broken hearts,
Piss against the wall when drunk,
Abuse, seduce, ignore and amuse themselves.
New city, new life, new distraction.
The human race is still running,
Trampling underfoot with savage pace,
Ordered and civilised with concrete spirit and
Herbicide, pesticide and singular corroboration.

It's all the same bullshit, y'know

Éamonn Lynskey

Éamonn has had poems published in many magazines. He was nominated for the Sunday Tribune/Hennessy Literary Award for New Irish Poetry in 2006 and one of his poems will feature on the 2009 OXFAM calendar. His first collection Dispatches and Recollections was published in 1998 and he is currently working on his second, for publication by Seven Towers in winter 2009/2010. Éamonn, who holds a Diploma in Italian Language and Culture has also translated the works of modern Italian poets into English. He is also a long time contributor to the open mic scene in Dublin. The following two poems are by Éamonn.

The Bookstalls at Stazione Termini, Rome

(for Arcidio Baldani, poet, dates unknown)

Down the road from Termini the bookstalls
and their ancient owners husband out
their days. Such piles of old forgotten classics,
mounds of dog-eared fascist magazines —
Such endless mouldering stacks of sad remainders
of that literary past where poets
thought that poetry could save the world,
then suffered through two wars that proved them wrong.

This man has spread his paper on a batch
of yellowed war reports. This woman smokes
among her pornographic videos.
And here a stall stands unattended
while its owner steps across the road
for coffee – But a friend has sidled in
behind the bargain Petrarchs and Pascolis
in case I might intend to make a purchase.

Dieci mila buyes the 'Poesie'
of Arcidio Baldani (nineteen
seventy-five) — The tenth of the three hundred
autographed, with letters of reply
from notables, including Perugia's bishop
thanking but declining comment since
he is a churchman and not critic, but
is pleased to find the poems 'ampi', 'profondi'

Where are you, my mirror image, now
Arcidio? (although I haven't fallen
to such letters, yet.) A gravestone? Or
just old in some apartment block with cat
and kettle and long shelves of books
you'll never read again? I never met you,
but I think I know you well. Your verses
yearn for permanence, (that charlatan)

in face of flux (that tyrant). Every night
you bolt your windows to the noisy world
that rushes past you, fast as that few years
when Mussolini led men to believe
that things would change — His speeches heaped up
in these bookstalls here in quantities
as vast as his ambition and as unread
as our poems, Arcidio. And look! —

Here under tourist guides and atlases
an old anthology in bad repair
but housing all the greats: Montale, Saba-
House we called on often, you and I,
unstoppable our urge to recreate
the world in words! I'm calling still, still browsing
in the bookstalls, sitting out the evening
into night. And sometimes writing something
like these lines for you Arcidio, for us.

Elegy for the Philadelphia Wireman (d. 1982?)

His work was found by chance one trash night
in a Philadelphia sidestreet by
a someone wasn't looking for it –
Dead, or moved away, the wireman
left no forwarding address, just
these twelve pieces made
from discards, twisted, bent, persuaded
to yield something of the soul
they never had until his hands
pressed down on them and woke it:

skeletal umbrellas, batteries, pens
and nuts and bolts and wardrobe hangers,
coils of red and black electric cable
writhing skyward – Gesturing
despair? Or supplicating mercy? This
the art, the making of the thing,
the thing allowed to speak its heart,
without the artist intervening (and
no photographs, no anecdotes, no
long explanatory notes). This

the art, the what-remains-behind
to be the sole begetter of itself,
its poor creator gone to meet his own,
bequeathing this the most the valuable
the artefact could ever hope for:
absence of its maker and
the freedom to be beautiful despite
his ugliness, wise despite
his crass stupidities, exemplar
of the kindnesses he knew a lifetime

hopelessly locked up inside him and
could show out only in these tapestries
and loops of interwoven wire,
these nails, these coins, these watches, tools
and jewellery bound by rubber bands
and tape. And even then could show out
only if we found them in that skip
before the trashmen took it. Even then
and only if we weren't looking for them.
Only if we found them just by chance.

Donal Moloney

Donal Moloney was born 1976 and comes from Waterford. He has been writing seriously for ten years, during which time he has written a novel, several novellas and many short stories and poems. He is currently completing a collection of three novellas. He works as a freelance translator and lives in Dublin.
He is a regular featured reader at both Chapters and Verse Reading Series and The Last Wednesday Reading and Open Mic Series.

Excerpt from *The Mask*

There was a single long, narrow corridor. The roof was low and intermittently he had to stoop. The moist air was refreshingly cool on his skin. Troubling him, however, was violent heartburn from the chilli con carne. The coolness bathing his skin in conjunction with the darkness and silence accentuated the burning fantastically and gave him the unnerving feeling of being bodiless except for a great flaming heart. The tongued-and-grooved planking on the floor of the tunnel bore the traces of recent sweeping. Set into the walls at shoulder height at intervals of about ten yards were little recesses with blackened metal brackets, presumably for torches. He came to a section where the roof bulged down, forcing him to get down on his hunkers and duck-walk five yards. Beyond that, there were small cavernous rooms on either side containing wine casks. He entered the second of these on his right and paused to take stock of his feelings. He felt his heart thump amid the flaming; there was some excitement. But there was little sense of wonder. His emotions were in no way commensurate to the moment. To stir up some extra anticipation, he shut his eyes and imagined the unknown statue to which so many people had been sacrificed.

He took out the hammer and chisel. The cement binding the stones in the back wall of the chamber was easily loosened. Within five minutes he had ascertained there was indeed another chamber behind this one; within twenty he was in the second chamber. He had proceeded according to plan, taking pains to avoid the wall collapsing or the stones becoming overly chipped. He picked up the largest of the loose chippings lying in the first chamber and put them in the second, then spread the dust around with his foot. With considerable exertion, he then rearranged the casks so that three of them stood a little in front of the breach, concealing it. Next, he chiselled an opening in the back wall of the second chamber, and within fifteen minutes was standing in the third chamber. From here on, due to the experience gained and the fact that progressively less care had to be taken to preserve the stones and dampen the noise, things went very quickly. In a further fifty minutes he was standing in the seventh chamber, behind whose rear wall, according to Guerrero, the statue should stand. Again he paused. This time the excitement was more palpable, but his rapid, hurdling advance gave him the unsettling impression of existing in two times at once: one, the sharp, striding time of his progress; lagging behind, the time of wonderment. He felt there was no way of reconciling them now by waiting. Surely the statue of Huitzilipochtli, the presence of the absent-faced terror of his childhood, would achieve that union of times with instant violence. He would have liked to have felt a little fear, but the heartburn and chiselling labour had put paid to that.

On he went. More chiselling, removing of stones, a peek, and there stood Huitzilipochtli huge and gleaming in the centre of the eighth chamber.

He grinned as a wave of euphoria passed through him, a sense of satisfaction, well-being, an appreciation of his cleverness and fortune. He slowly removed the remaining stones needed to make a gap big enough to fit through, savouring the moment, stopping often to compulsively shine the torch on the idol. He thought of the newspaper headlines, the interviews, the immortality such an extraordinary find would assure him. He even imagined the colourfulness of the story would win him proverbial fame, that grocers and housewives would come to know his name. Most of all, he thought of how this achievement would be snugly embedded in respect. If he had the choice, he would donate the statue to the Mexican National Anthropological Museum. Even if it wasn't up to him, he was certain – seeing as he was clearly the sole finder and would display munificence in word and deed throughout – that he would get great recognition and acclaim. Guillermo Guerrero would also become a household name.

Huitzilipochtli – only depicted in a few codices and of whom only one known small statue was extant. How did he look on the top of the pyramid in the Templo Mayor? As terrifying as he had imagined as a child? Or unimposing enough to explain Cortes's sangfroid in informing Montezuma before the statue that his god was a devil and asking permission to place a statue of the Virgin on the altar?

He climbed in through the hole and approached the statue, slowly circling it, trying to absorb its actuality with his gaze. The statue was awesome. It was about three metres tall yet squat, squatly and squarely robust. It was made of basalt, but this was only visible in patches through the abundance of jewels inlaid all over the body and out-glistening the humbler stone. The jewels were of a great variety, with green and blue stones predominating, and arranged harmoniously. There was a thin coating of dust in places, and thick cobwebs spanned joints and crooks. There were also tiny splotches of a white substance, which had they not been so small, he would have trusted his first impression in taking to be bird droppings. Twining thickly round the body in relief were six giant snakes. On closer inspection the carvings he initially thought depicted scales looked more like feathers. He alternately saw them as scales and as feathers, depending on his standpoint as he circled. When he perceived them as scales, he could almost hear slithering, their terribly rough abrasion against the stony body of the god. When he imagined them as feathers, he could hear a too-rapid ruffling, as if swift, evil movements were taking place constantly just outside his field of vision. The jaws of the snakes resembled beaks, though the black obsidian fangs were truly serpentine in their menace. The hollow, stony eyes reinforced the essence of human fear of this beast – not of any predatoriness, but of arbitrariness.

Hanging around the statue's neck were actual human skulls and heart-shaped pieces of gold and silver. In its right hand it held a round shield made of gold, on the face of which there was a turquoise mosaic. Out of either side of the shield there protruded the bases and heads of four arrows, also gold, the fletchings rendered in intricate detail, the nocks double and suggestive of claws. In its left hand it held a fantastically long silver sword. The blade was broad near the hilt but tapered extremely gradually to a tiny point. Feather motifs were finely worked two-thirds of the way down its length. The last third was dyed black and recalled the long beak of a wader or hummingbird. Projecting from both sides of the blade at irregular intervals were flames, all tilting backward, creating the illusion that the sword was surging forward. At some points the flames still had traces of the red dye they must originally have been painted with. The whole flaming sword-bird, for all its intricacy and intrinsic unnaturalness, was executed with flair and conviction, the artist having captured in his mind the essence of a flaming sword-bird and reproduced it as naturally as if it were a face.

The legs were short in relation to the torso. In place of the left foot there was a snake's head, this one fangless and with its jaws open wide. No jewels drew attention to this aspect, and the basalt snakehead gaping meanly where the foot should have been troubled the eye. On the arms and legs were traces of blue colouring. Another notable feature of the statue was the deep rectangular hollow carved into the centre of the chest, in which a heart of green jadeite stood.

The head was free from adornment, which gave it an imposing presence. The lips of the large mouth were turned down in a grimace. The nose was broad and somewhat flat and slightly crooked at the bridge as if it had once been broken, though it still projected a sense of extreme vigour. Indents did for eyes, and set deep inside them, odd in the absence of the rest of the irises and almost entirely obscured in shadow, were small, smooth black obsidians for pupils. They expressed a deep melancholy, but also a grim resoluteness. They were the eyes of someone whom fate has been unkind to, who has retreated from misfortune to accept only a humble, brutish role in the affairs of humankind, someone whose better aspects have been denied and who has gathered all these suppressed potentialities deep inside him and applied this surplus violently to the only role he has been allowed, his eyes saying, 'So I am this then, then let me be this and only this and on and on until you all weep.' In their black obsidian centre, however, the eyes were impenetrable, the torchlight being deflected by the tiny stones.

The statue seemed to have a helmet on, one similar to the morion helmets the conquistadors wore, but on inspecting it from the back, he discovered that the forceful head was actually shown emerging from the beak of a bird. He couldn't see the bird's body. He walked back round the front and stepped back a few paces. From here, he saw that the statue as a whole could be seen as a man emerging from the body of a bird. Apart from the head coming out of the bird's head, this effect was achieved by simple feather-like carvings running down the statue's sides. From this distance, the overall impression of the warrior-bird-god was breathtaking. There was no doubt that this was the missing statue of Huitzilipochtli. This was what had confronted the victims at the top of the pyramid steps.

He was interested by the statue, yet perfectly in control of himself. It was as if an invisible barrier separated him from fascination, from wonder, from fear. He imagined he felt tremors, shivers up his spine, but these were phenomena he could observe detached. He circled and circled, felt it with his hands, directed the torch to individual details. He told himself now was the time to go back, burst into the museum, make his announcement and wait for the media sensation. Yet something stubborn inside him wanted to feel the momentousness of his find in this solitary intimacy, instead of being just distantly conscious of it. He insisted to himself that he had felt enough, that this is what one feels, but he wanted more.

He slumped down in a corner and began looking around the room, his eyes scanning the space for something else, despite there being obviously nothing: it was a square room with stone walls, empty except for the statue in the middle. He looked at the statue, which had lost all charm for him. He felt like he was in a museum and was ready to move on to the next exhibit, the next sensation. He had assimilated the statue as much as he was capable of, had cross-checked its features against those mentioned in Guerrero's description. A restlessness grew within him, a desire for an unknown find beyond this one. This desire ran up against the manifest emptiness of the room. The upshot was his getting down on his hands and knees and crawling around the periphery of the room, pawing at the walls for some hidden recess.

This went on for twenty minutes, at the end of which he sat back down enraged and humiliated. A petulance overcame him, and he muttered swears in Spanish, cursing the room and the god. Again he resolved to leave, and again he was retained by an indeterminate wish. He took out the hammer and chisel and began chipping away at the stone in the back wall until he broke through to the next chamber. How many chambers were there? A quick look round this one convinced him of its emptiness, so he immediately set to chipping away at the back wall in what, his growing tiredness notwithstanding, was degenerating into a frenzy. Penetrating the wall, he entered the following chamber, and here there was something – in the back wall there was an alcove at chest height containing three objects: a bowl, a manuscript and a mask.

Each glowed with its own discrete appeal in the alternating torchlight. He recognised the bowl as a cuauhxicalli – the vessel in which the Aztecs placed the freshly extracted hearts of their victims. It was made of stone, and embossed on the outside was a wreath of feathers and below that a circle of unlinked rings. Its inside was blackened, with an amber-coloured stain at the bottom. The mask was silver and spare. It had slightly larger than life-size holes for eyes, a broad even slit for a mouth and a rudimentary triangular protrusion with nostril holes for a nose. The ears were pierced. It was a realistic depiction of a face, though given only the most basic of features. The face conveyed no emotion, no inner life whatsoever. Knowing from the early art efforts of his own children that giving a face emotion is not only easy but almost unavoidable, he wondered what kind of uncanny imagination had created the mask. Yet it was precisely this lack of detail that lent the mask its stark aura and which in the instant it captured his imagination swallowed it whole.

Uncontrollably and in a way which could not be fully accounted for by what he had found, he began to tremble. Indeed there was something fateful and ghastly about finding three such objects on what looked like an altar, but surely this was part of the plan set out by Guerrero. However, following the internal logic of his progression, this was what he had been looking for, and he found not wonder but terror. His heartburn was now waning, but slowly and horribly. It felt as if his heart had reached maximum conflagration and was now coldly dying. He imagined an accumulation of ash.

He snatched up Guerrero's manuscript, which was crudely bound in black leather. Now – to finally discover what the madman had in mind. He sat down against the wall to his left (such that the wall with the recess was on his left) and read with a lucidity proportionate to his desperate conviction that the book was the only possible antidote to his terror. Alone in this dark room with his heart turning to ash, it seemed unreasonable to him that he should suffer so, senseless that he be brought to this house of darkness. His suffering railed against the apparent meaninglessness of it being he who had come to this place. The book had to yield an explanation.

The book was called *La Oferta* and was a novel. It was written in an elegant, neat hand, geometric in its regularity. Quickly it became clear to him that this was a very different Guerrero to that of *La Noche Triste*. The many strands of the story interlaced smartly, creating an ever thicker weave of meaning. The characters became increasingly charged, and, after a point, every paragraph crackled with destinies colliding. Everywhere there was sin, everywhere the sound of brittle souls snapping. The protagonist, whom on a dispassionate appraisal of his actions an objective observer would qualify as basically good, is shown as bludgeoning his way through the world, chipping away at the happiness of those he meets, and consequently, inversely, the reader sees his soul flake away. The novel was packed with poems, aphorisms and historical and mythological allusions. Its psychological acuity was extreme, as was the emotional complexity of the interactions of the characters. Although the third-person narrator's tone was neutral and tolerant, there was a rigour to how actions had consequences, effects all the more implacable for having worked their way undiminished through the convolutions of human affairs. The end saw the protagonist take a black obsidian knife and carve out his heart, dropping it pink and still beating on the Mexican flag laid out on his kitchen table before his disheartened body walks through the city directly to an underground cellar, descends, floats through wall after wall, passing the great missing statue of Huitzilipochtli, which shudders at the sight of it, and climbs up into an alcove between a cuauhxicalli and a silver mask, contorting itself elaborately and unnaturally to fit into the space, leaving time to decay it like a bat that has died in its sleep.

He read the novel, which was two hundred and twenty pages long, with uncommon concentration aided by the focus of the torchlight on the damp, foxed pages. It was only an antidote to his terror insofar as the plot distracted him from it. But every few paragraphs there was a whiplash sentence slinging him back into the bleakness. Although the novel was full of descriptions, he was incapable of compressing the words to make an agreeable image bloom in his mind. A jagged ferocity in the language kept puncturing the story and returning him to his ashen heart and trembling body. He knew he was too weak to move, that it was impossible for him to leave the place so roundly defeated that his past and future had been snagged in its cogs. He had to find a way out in these pages. He did not look around him once, did not want to see the bowl and the mask in all their unyieldingness. Whenever he lifted his eyes from the page it was to rest his gaze on his shaking knees. Eventually it was sleep which came and struck the blow that released him

He awoke groggy and stiff but in sure command of his emotions. The torch still shone, though dimly, and he realised he should leave quickly before the batteries ran out. Now in control of himself, he was also in control of the room and its objects. He smiled at the terror of the previous day – dark, cavernous rooms, giant statue of a pagan god, vessel for receiving the hearts of human sacrifices, mysterious manuscript. All these things had had their effect on him. Although he had clung to Guerrero's manuscript before falling asleep, he now felt a huge hatred for the man for having put him through such an ordeal. He knew his terror was not necessarily the effect Guerrero had been aiming for, but this Guerrero had made him look foolish, even if only to himself. Revenge would be easy: he would tear up the manuscript, or, better still, burn it.

He would go now to the National Anthropological Museum. If it was night, he would return to his hotel and go straight to the museum after breakfast. He had no real idea how long he had been in the cellar. He wedged the manuscript into his bag with a malevolent smile, then looked over at the alcove. An idea flashed through his mind. He walked over and picked up the mask, then put it up to his face. It was an approximate fit. He then placed it right up against his skin and slowly removed his hand from it. It stayed balanced on his face. He tilted his head forward. On reaching an angle of about 45 degrees, the mask fell off. He put it back on. It was pretty uncomfortable and heavy, but it fit and, if he kept his head upright and walked carefully, would stay on. He could see through the eyeholes and breathe through the nostrils and mouth-slit. His nose fit tolerably well into the mask nose. He puckered his lips into a massive smirk. What an idea! He would walk through the streets of Mexico City and straight up to the National Anthropological Museum wearing an Aztec mask. This would be the audacity to set the whole brouhaha in motion. What style! Now he was on form!

He left the room, empty but for the vessel sitting untouched on the ledge of the alcove. In the next room he did a little dance around Huitzilipochtli, and now saw the mighty god as inanimate, unmenacing jewels and stone which would bring him fame. He walked through chamber after chamber. When he got to the first chamber, he tilted and turned the casks on their chimes right up to the breach, covering it to show no signs of an incursion. He walked down the long corridor, imagining the wine he would drink that night in celebration. Why, he would go to the restaurant above and drink a vintage from this very cellar! He climbed the iron ladder. To his great delight, the torch went out. He pushed open the trapdoor and his crown was bathed in sunlight.

Joe Moran

Joe is a sculptor and artist from East Wall in Dublin, where he still lives. Among his public art works is The Family Group sculpture in Fairview Park in Dublin. Joe is a full member of the Temple Bar Gallery Studios. The following poem is by Joe.

It was just after the postman came

That morning – I will never forget it
For our lives were changed forever

      She got up from the table
      To get the morning's post.
      When she came back to the kitchen
      I asked as I always did
      Is there something for me today?

I did not get the usual answer of 'who would be writing to you?'
I waited for her to say that – she did not,
I looked at her – no words,
Her eyes told me there was something wrong,
I thought to myself 'what to do?'
'play it down?'
for I had an idea there was something wrong;
she did not know I knew
she had been to the hospital
      I had heard it on the answer machine
so when she said on the day she was to go to the hospital
      I asked her where are you going today
She said 'with a friend for coffee'
I did not say I knew about the hospital.
I sat for what seems to me to be a long time
But it was not,
I got up and walked across the kitchen
To where she was standing with the official looking paper still in her hand
I thought 'why do people send letters of this kind so official?'
I did not look at the letter – I did not want to know what was in it,
What is wrong, I asked,
Nothing, she said,
I know there is something up, what is it?
Tell me what is in the letter you have in your hand.
She still did not say a word,
I could not tell her I knew about the hospital,
I can see it in your eyes.
She said: there is nothing for you to know about it
It is just women's problems.
But it was not women's problems, it was ours,

I could not tell her I knew about the hospital.
I should have taken her in my arms and kissed her and told her that I loved
      her
To do as I would have when I was eighteen,
That was so long ago, for we are now past all that at fifty,
I thought,
What has gone wrong with us, we think too much.
I looked into her eyes, you could cut the silence with a knife,
I said, 'now listen to me, it's not that bad'
But I should have kissed her.

Anne Morgan

Anne was born in London and grew up in Dublin. She studied English at St. Patrick's college, Maynooth. Anne has done readings in the Ballymun Axis Theatre and the Irish Writers Centre and has had work published in *Newsfour*, *Riposte* and *Electric Acorn*. The following two poems are by Anne.

Listening to Opera

I did not really understand
I was more excited by my present
An apron
Than the new arrival

When my mother told me
That you were for me
That you were my baby
I was thrilled

I watched you grow
I looked after you
Now you look after me

Travelling in Japan
You are seeing a world I never knew
While I brew tea in Ireland

I am in touch with you instantly
Through the flick of a mouse
Thought I would miss you more

Listening to Opera
I am discovering new things too

Fallen Angel

(From Roddy Doyle to Elizabeth Barrett Browning)

Not much peace
In your lifetime
Not much peace
Now

Children still neglected
Still unhappiness
I have regrets

Born in the Bronx
A lowly schoolteacher
Till I made it big
Got high on caffeine
As I battled with words

You battled with words
Too
Battled with song
And with verse
In a man's world

Struggled for identity
Not just a woman
But a poet

Noel Ó Briain

Noel Ó Briain was born in Kerry, grew up in Dublin and now lives in Camolin, Wexford. He is a playwright and poet and a former head of drama at RTE. He has worked for many years in theatre, radio and television as an actor, producer/ director, designer and script editor. He produced and directed many plays in the Damer Hall under the auspices of Gael Linn. He also designed the sets for many other productions. He won a National Jacob's Award for his production and adaptation of Seán Ó Tuama's Judas Iscariot agus a Bhean. His poetry and short stories have been published in a number of literary magazines including The Kilkenny Magazine and Poetry Ireland. They have also been broadcast on radio in the short story slot and on Sunday Miscellany. His first collection *Scattering Day, 21 Sonnets and Other Poems* was published by Seven Towers in 2007. The following playlet is by Noel.

ÁINLE AND ÁRDÁN ARE ALREADY DEAD

A Playlet

This playlet was inspired by John Millington Synge's great dramatic tragedy,

DEIRDRE OF THE SORROWS (with a nod to the original myth).

Áinle and Árdán are minor characters in Synge's play; so peripheral to the action in Deirdre's and Naoise's love story as to be almost nonexistent.

So while all this high drama was going on around them, what was Áinle's and Árdán's 'take' on the situation? Were they just passive onlookers? Voyeurs, even? Or did they develop an understanding of what love is and its consequences?

In a way, this short play is a re-telling of the *DEIRDRE* story but as seen through the eyes of Naoise's brothers.

CHARACTERS
ÁRDÁN
ÁINLE

They are brothers
ÁINLE is the younger. He takes life as he finds it, a day at a time.
He is impetuous.

ÁRDÁN's resentment and frustration at having been forced into exile has built up over the years.
He tolerates his brother's impetuousness.

PRONUNCIATION
The rhythm and assonance of the dialogue is based on the Gaelic names being pronounced as follows: (The stress normally falls on the first syllable).

ÁRDÁN	AWR / DAWN
ÁINLE	AWN / LUH
NAOISE	NEE / SHUH
CONCHUBAR	CRUH / HOOR
DEIRDRE	DARE / DRUH
EMAIN MACHA	OW / 'N (as in crown) MOCKA
SLIABH FUADH	SHLEEVE / FOOAH
ALBAN (Scotland)	OL uh* BUN

* In Gaelic pronunciation an auxiliary vowel is added between certain consonants. (pronounced like the neutral vowel sound in English.)

ÁINLE AND ÁRDÁN ARE ALREADY DEAD

SCENE: On a seashore somewhere in Alban
TIME: The Past
DARKNESS.
THE SOUND OF SLOW, OMINOUS DRUM BEATS, HEAVY AT FIRST,
THEN FADING AS THE LIGHT COMES UP AND WE HEAR THE SOUND OF WAVES
BREAKING ON THE SHORE.
ÁINLE and ÁRDÁN are standing on the seashore in the slanting evening sunlight,
looking out West towards Ireland. (i.e. towards the audience)
ÁINLE is elated, glad to be leaving Scotland after their seven years in exile.
ÁRDÁN, however, is in a more desultory mood.

ÁINLE
That went well.

They continue looking out towards the sea.

      Conchubar is not the worst.
The deal is fair, think you?

ÁRDÁN does not reply.

          Safe passage first,
And then our lands and stock returned in Emain;
A deal that bears the royal seal of The Crown.

He looks at his brother but ÁRDÁN just continues staring out to sea.

Seven years in exile to the day.
And now, dear brother, we are on our way.

At last he notes ÁRDAN'S desultory mood.

Have we not heard the call of Conchubar's drum;
Deirdre and Naoise too. *(He laughs)* Then why so glum?

ÁRDÁN
I do not trust Conchubar. I've heard that beat.
I fear it is the sounding of defeat,

ÁINLE

Seven years is a lonely lifetime, brother,
Seven years and we have known no other.

ÁRDÁN

More an Eternity. Alban's no place
For the Sons of Usna. Was our fate
Not destined by the gods for greater glory
Than stand and watch unfold our brother's story
With dark haired Deirdre, though the gods did frown;
For 'twas foretold her fate lay with the crown
As Conchubhar's mate and queen; not mistress of
Our brother, Naoise, and forbidden love.

ÁINLE tries to divert ÁRDÁN from this line of conversation.

ÁINLE

A High King's word is good enough for me.
We sail for Ireland, Árdán. We are free.

But ÁRDÁN will not be diverted.

ÁRDÁN

Free!

Resentment, repressed for years, now comes out.

                  And seven years in exile thrust
Upon us. Think you, brother, that was just!

ÁINLE

Passion, not cold justice was the cause.
When lovers meet in heat there are no laws.

ÁRDÁN can no longer contain his pent up frustration.

ÁRDÁN

And all the while, dear Áinle, as they lay
In hotted flesh did we not have to play
The eunuch; or our lust abate alone,
Or splay some Alban slut as cold as stone?
We sought the strong camaraderie of men.
Some laughed and said it was beyond their ken;

Then, sublimation, where there was no other,
Drew close together brother unto brother.

ÁINLE is taken aback but tries to revert to the subject of their departure.

ÁINLE
Why say you then that Naoise now will go?
Did not Conchubar send messengers before?

ÁRDÁN
Wee mad Owen with a crack a mile wide in his skull!
Brave Fergus now and pardons for all in full.
These self same terms now offered by Conchubar
Have come from Emain with every overture.

He shakes his head.
I like it not. I do not trust the man.

ÁINLE
Yet Naoise and now Deirdre's for the plan.

ÁRDÁN
Deirdre! Aye. Aye, Deirdre is the one!

ÁINLE
A King's pardon is no small thing to shun.
And why would Naoise go? He is no fool.

ÁRDÁN
I know not yet. I fear he's but a tool
In Conchubar's scheme. What scheme I know not yet.
Conchubar wants Deirdre as his Queen. He's set
His mind on that. He will not be denied.
If truth be told, then right is on his side.

ÁINLE can hardly believe his brother is saying this.

It was our brother broke the kinsman's trust
And exiled brothers for a brother's lust.
The gods had destined Deirdre for Conchubar.
For seven years this role he did endure
The shameful role of cuckold King in Emain

And brought that ignominy on Ulster's Crown.
He seeks revenge for every slur and slight;
Will bring to bear all Emain's power and might
To free Dark Deirdre from our brother's arms.
Believe me, Áinle, I hear clear alarms.

ÁINLE

And, yet, 'tis clear our Naoise hears no bells.

ÁRDÁN

Then he is doomed! And you and I as well.

ÁINLE

And what of Deirdre of the raven hair
This seven years lay in our brother's lair?

ÁRDÁN

She is for Conchubar. Gods are not mocked.
Snatched almost from her mother's womb and locked
Away where only females would be seen
And raised to be Royal Ulster's chosen Queen;
Hidden high on the west slopes of Sliabh Fuadh
Where no man but Conchubar would come to woo her.
But Naoise came upon the girl by chance,
Stripped to bathe her milk white skin. One glance
And all the gods above could not deny
The blood's red race desire to satisfy.
But gods can wait for all eternity.
They are not mocked; they wait for destiny;
Slow destiny that will not be denied.
The Sons of Usna have already died.

ÁINLE takes ÁRDÁN's hand and places it against his breast.

ÁINLE

Touch me, brother, we are much alive.
Though eunuchs now, in Emain we shall take wives.

He clasps ÁRDÁN.
See, brother, we are flesh. (*He kisses him*) See how we feel.
Do spirits kiss?
He draws his sword.

122 ————————

                    As long as I have steel

Conchubar and all his men shall be no threat
To Naoise or to Árdán or to -

ÁRDÁN (*interrupting*)
                                          Yet
I fear Conchubar. I fear he has some scheme.
And I fear Deirdre too.

ÁINLE, who is re-sheathing his sword looks up, surprised.

                         She had a dream
That love, her love and Naoise's love would last.
Now she has deep fears that that is past.

ÁINLE again looks surprised.

Look not surprised. I see it in her eyes
Whose shining brightness did outmatch the sky's.
Each month the moon doth wane in her own time,
And, yet, the full moon once again will climb.
And woman too will have her monthly ways
Knowing, like the moon, 'tis but a phase.
But when love wanes there is no phased return.
With love's decline, no fire again shall burn.
Now Deirdre fears that Naoise's love has waned
And wonders if 'tis what the gods ordained
For disobedience. And yet when first
They came to Alban's shores how they did thirst
To sip each other; never satisfied;
Unquenchable; and how Dark Deirdre cried
Aloud and moaned and begged for Naoise's thrust
And called his name again, again. Their lust
Unbridled knew no bounds nor night from day,
Heaven from earth, such was their ecstasy.

ÁRDÁN has become lost in his own thoughts but now turns back to ÁINLE.
Have we not watched them race without a stitch
Through fields and fall and couple in a ditch;
Or through the woods of Alban and then see
Naoise plant his Deirdre 'gainst a tree,
A sturdy oak; and yet the branches quivered

As they beat leather, trembled, moaned and shivered.
Then Deirdre would go down at Naoise's shout
And suck his manhood with her blood red mouth.
The brothers look at each other for a moment.

Now she has seen love's moon in its last phase
And knows there is no new moon. These are days
Of reckoning. She will not wait to see
The light go dim in Naoise's eyes and be
A dying ember of what once was fire
That burned through her soul with deep desire.
Rather would she have it Naoise died
And Áinle and Árdán dead by his side
Than watch love fade where love once dwelled
As morning sun the morning mist dispels.

They are silent for a moment.

Deirdre has decided we should go
Not Naoise. And yet she must surely know
Conchubar cannot be trusted; that his word
Is not his bond but rather that his sword
Shall send the Sons of Usna to their graves.

ÁINLE
Pray tell, shall Deirdre die; shall she be brave?

ÁRDÁN
Not she. For 'tis decreed that she shall wed
Conchubar; and grief shall claim the nuptial bed.
The gods take strange revenge on mortals who
Would try to circumvent what they must do.

ÁINLE
For us, dear brother, tell me, is there more;
Know you now what have the gods in store?

ÁRDÁN
It was foretold ere you and I were born
Usna's sons should die tomorrow morn.

ÁINLE
In Emain Macha?

ÁRDÁN
                    That is my belief.

ÁINLE
Then let us stay in Alban. No more grief.
Let us thwart the gods; beg Naoise stay
And give to Conchubar Deirdre as his lay.

ÁRDÁN
The gods cannot be thwarted. It is writ
That we shall die in Emain. It is fit.
ÁINLE
Has man no say in his own destiny?
Must he be subject to some Deity
That he has never known? Let us remain
In Alban. You have said the gods ordained
That we shall die in Emain. Then let us stay
And circumvent the gods this very day.
Stand and show that you and I can hold
Our Fate in our own hands if we be bold.

ÁRDÁN is bemused at his brother's impetuosity.

ÁRDÁN
Brave words, dear Áinle. Would that it were so.
Come, dear brother, come now let us go.

ÁINLE
No! I would rather die by my own hand
In Alban though it be a stranger's land.
It is not death I fear. I shall not bow
To Destiny. No gods shall tell me how
Or where I die. I give you Áinle's word.
Suddenly he draws his sword.
See, my brother, see I draw my sword.

He proffers the sword to ÁRDÁN

Take it. Hold it firm. Now give me yours.
Then let us run and run each other through.
ÁRDÁN again just smiles wearily at ÁINLE's zealousness.

ÁRDÁN
Sheath your blade, dear brother, sheath your blade.
He takes ÁINLE's sword, re-sheaths it in the scabbard.
THE HEAVY SOUND OF DRUMBEATS ARE HEARD AGAIN BUT THIS TIME RISING
TO A CRESCENDO UNDER ÁRDAN'S FINAL SPEECH
THE SOUND OF THE SEA DIES OUT.
We shall die, but we shall not be laid
In Alban for the gods must have their way.
No, dear brother, no, we cannot stay.
We shall die in Emain, die as men,
As brothers, Áinle, Árdán, Naoise, then
A story full of wonder shall be told
How the Sons of Usna ne'er grew old.

They embrace each other.
THE DRUMBEATS HAVE REACHED A CRESENDO
THEY STOP ABRUPTLY

SILENCE.
CURTAIN OR BLACKOUT

Tommy Frank O'Connor

Tommy Frank O'Connor has a number of books in print, including a poetry collection *Attic Warpipes* (Bradshaw Books, 2005), a novel for children, *Kee Kee Cup & Tok* (WynkindeWorde, 2004), a novel for adults, *The Poacher's Apprentice* (Marino, 1997) and two collections of short stories *Pulse* and *Loose Head* both published by Doghouse Books. Tommy Frank is a member of the Irish Writers Union and of The Society of Irish Playwrights, and is on the Poetry Ireland panel of Writers in schools. In this capacity he conducts residencies in schools, prisons and libraries. He is current writer in residence in Kerry. The following two poems are by Tommy Frank.

EVE

And the Lord God Almighty, thinking
it was not well that Adam should roam
Alone, searching for what he did not know,
Anaesthetised him in a thicket.

Then inside the quiet of Adam's slumber
The God and maker of all things took a rib
From just above the sleeping man's hip
And with his breath called forth Woman.

Dreams awoke to sight of human vision
A creature like himself yet somehow different
A curve of hip, a waist of racing whippet,
And further up two nipple-budded bosoms.

And the Lord God Almighty, sensing
That his latest work was near perfection
Named her *Eve* to Adam's introduction
And promised them their prize, with one precept —

They must not touch or take the tempting
Fruit of just one tree He called the apple —
All else in Eden's garden they could sample —
For just one day, as well as their own antics.

Then the tree, hitherto half-hidden,
with scent of apple blossom, summoned them
and a tempting serpent, quite unbidden
spun that first lie into their innocence

reluctant Adam wrestled with his thoughts
while Eve already knew what she was after
she plucked an apple, took that tempting bite
and found them both consigned to the hereafter.

CASTLEISLAND MEJ'UM

Well over half of a pint glass, in fact
Almost all the way there, it came into the world
Because no man's man could be seen sat
Behind a half-pint measure, that was for girls
Or ladies home from Boston or such parts.

Castleisland man, if he were to take his wife
Into a public house, left her in the snug,
Where a glass of porter, fortified
With a port or sherry, was deemed to be enough.
If she sat up at the counter alongside —
The brazen hussy surely should be churched.
Even with a group of other women
She could not go into a public house
Without reason; a funeral, or on business,
Minding money for their men-folk, or about
The price of sundries traded at the fair.

Meanwhile, up at the counter in their ways
Man-to-man important tales were bartered:
The deeds and heroes of their fathers' days
Were told and told again with new bits added;
Faction fights, how many skulls were cracked by whom;
Tossing the sheaf or throwing the heavy weights;

The half-hour deadlocked tug of war, that once
Was just a quarter, when the Parish Priest
Cut the rope lest the men of war collapse;
And fabled journeys to All-Irelands of the past.
Castleisland mediums always at the ready
A Fair Day in the town could not be thirsty.

Mel O'Dea

Mel O'Dea is an artist living in Cork. Mel studied chemistry at Durham University and started her career in the sciences inventing, manufacturing and testing Microchips for University College Cork. She began her artistic career in earnest in 2000, following a period at the Byam Shaw School of Art in North London. The following poem is by Mel.

Untitled

I saw myself in the mirror of things — describing my thoughts and weaving
       them . . .
I wrapped the blanket around me to ward off the chill, the
Shart pags of frost, describing their art on the bedroom windows, moving
    through
Crisp moments, and the walking through leaves that
Portrayed the death of their memory, that existed through each story told on
Fireside evenings through which we come together to realise how apart
    we are, the
Voice of some foreign language eases in, we understand it, we
Move to describe each translation as it happened, the interchange of
    experience that
Fell snow-soft on the brow, the move through each consideration,
    through the stations, like a train, like the
Perpetual movement that taught us to dance before we became still,

    and taught us to dance again.

Edward O'Dwyer

Edward is a poet from Limerick. His work has featured in journals and anthologies. The following two poems are by Edward.

Hand in Hand

The answer is certainly yes,
but let me explain.

We are each other's everyday reminders
of how old we've gotten,
and in so little time.
Of all that we've lost
which can never be found.

We are mirrors and images – interchangeable –
of guilts and failures, inadequacies
that over the years became us.

So to answer your question,
of course I regret loving you.
Of course I do
when this is what you are.

But yet I feel
I've loved you more and more each day
and still do as the days pass.

To think, after forty years,
we still hold hands when we talk
more comfortably that ever doing so now . . .
our hands would seem to fit
in each other's
only as well as loves with regrets –

two like us
walking always hand in hand.

Wrinkle

Like a lining of
flesh-peeling barbed wire
topping high walls,
she rubbed and smoothed on
the creams and lotions daily.

Like giving dogs
the sniff but not the taste
of raw meat
she was careful to avoid
too much time in the sun.

And like a routine of
setting the house alarm,
brushing her hair
in the mirror
 of her dresser before bed
gave security enough
to sleep in confidence
till the morning.

But the particular morning
in it, there he is
over the brow of her image
looting youth and beauty
like the silverware;
the trespasser,
behind her defences
goading her with his victory.

Fintan O'Higgins

Fintan is a writer from Dublin now living in Nottingham, where he is the Literary and New Works Manager at the Theatre Writing Partnership. The following two poems are by Fintan.

Lonely Ballad

They waded through coupons for make-up
  And vouchers came up to their calf
For nothing says "I have a girlfriend"
  Like buying a pint and a half.

He craved for the love of a woman
  And the social status that lent one
But since he had no girl to love him
  The poor man was forced to invent one.

Now nothing says "I have a girlfriend"
  Like buying a pint and a half
Or "Baby on Board" on your windscreen,
  Or pot pourri kept in your gaff.

So he bought her a mixer and spirit
  And called out "I'm here!" cross the floor
But no-one was waiting to hear it
  So he nodded and smiled at the door.

"Just tell her if anyone sees her
  I've just gone to get us some Snax,"
And he bought her a passion fruit Breezer
  And he guzzled it down in the jacks.

Every month he went shopping for tampons
  And Primrose Oil by the vial
And he smiled at the girl at the counter
  A patient and boyfriendish smile.

And every two weeks he bought condoms
  For six times a week they had sex.
"The girlfriend has womanly needs, don't you know
  And that's what the lady expects!"

(The girl in the chemist's who served him
  Was feeling forlorn and forsaken
And she sighed as she watched him walk out of the shop
  But sure what was the point? He was taken.)

So Haagen-Dasz filled up his freezer
      His cupboard contained Special K,
His bath filled with lavender, peaches and lime
      And springtime and ocean spray.

He bought a subscription to Cosmo,
      Bought camisoles, candles and cakes,
Considerate flowers and thoughtful surprises
      And Galaxys, Moments and Flakes.

He bought them from polished well-dressed girls
      Who smiled but who never flirted
For they thought that if he bought her L'Oreal things
      Then really she must have been worth it.

Things from Chanel and from Gucci,
      Things bought from Estee Lauder
To show he was going out with a girl
      And to prove to the world he adauder.

And CDs of Celine Dion
      Herbal teas and infusions and blends
And he bought her clothes and videos
      With various actors from *Friends*.

He paid for his Flakes and his city breaks
      For matching twin towel-sets paid he,
And he packed it all up in his sporty car
      And he took it back home to his bedsit.

He wept as he sat in his fragrant flat,
      A man and all alone.
Till he overexfoliated one day
      And scrubbed himself bare to the bone.

And when they finally found him
      It wasn't for several weeks;
It took that long for the stench to rise
      Through the Lancomes and through the Cliniques.

They waded through coupons for make-up
        And wet-wipes and scrunchies and jellies
And they found his bones smelling of pot pourri
        By a big stack of Cathy Kellys.

(And the girls in the chemist's and Body Shop
        And the make-up counter all noted
That they never again saw that nice young man
        With the girlfriend on whom he so doted.)

For Aifric, for Christmas

From when, in the white square of my shade,
> That shade before dawn-colour suffuses you, lily-of-the-valley, with that glow
> That burns like torchlight stirring the milky tendrils of a child's hand

To when, in that same square, the colour after violet sinks like neon light into the snow,
> Midmorning's yellow goes skittering on clouds' contours, framed in

blue;
> Green trees, red traffic lights, and me and you about town,
> Can feel the give and heft of the daylight's weave,
> And after the intoxicated twin purples of doubtful twilight leave,

the sky
> Rests. When the day diffuses, I hope it is I
>> In your fleecy dusk-clouds resting my thin orange crown,
> That resolved again in square and black and white,
> All the light's shades are contained in the night.

And, since the day - in that same white blind square -
The iris and translucence, the gleam of glass and mother-of-pearl are there,
Surely it also contains in its snow-sand white
The strip of absoluteness stretched between day and night,
The papery blackness of a cabin propped silhouette on sky;
Where lolloping forms on duny humps are filed,
Where the brightness is understood – in a silver square on card –
Of the jewels of pilgrims who are following a star
> Drawn by a child.

Christmas Eve, 2005

Maeve O'Sullivan

Dubliner Maeve O'Sullivan is a lecturer in journalism and an occasional broadcaster. She has had numerous poems and haiku published in various journals and is a former poetry winner at Lisstowel Writer's Week. A founder member of Haiku Ireland, Maeve's first haiku collection *Double Rainbow* (co-authored with Kim Richardson) was published in 2005 by Alba Publishers. She is a member of the Valentine Poetry Workshop. The following two poems are by Maeve.

Snowdonian

(following a visit to a disused copper mine in Sygun, North Wales)

For Nessa O'Mahony

Way down beneath the ground he digs for ore,
Six days in every week, ten hours a day.
The miner's life no longer than two score.

With hammer, chisel, pick he starts to bore
His way through tons of cuprous rock and clay,
Way down beneath the ground he digs for ore.

His yearly wage is twenty pounds and four,
The only extra break on Christmas Day.
A miner's life no longer than two score.

Waste rock and timber used to build each floor,
A candle on his helmet lights the way
As, down beneath the ground, he digs for ore.

Thin stalactites where water dripped before
And moss-green malachites are here to stay,
The miner's life no longer than two score.

A shaft of sunlight greets him at the door
Where sorted rocks are fathomed before pay
Back down beneath the ground he digs for ore,
The miner's life no longer than two score.

New Drumbeat

(after the Fleadh Cheoil in Listowel, August 2002)

And I thought I knew something
about rhythm, and the west.
Watching my first Clare Batterin', feet
feral on the floor of *The Harp and Lion*,
I understand that dancing is the reason
for all of these tunes; My hands try to keep time:
the left one toning the new drum's oily skin,

the right one moving the tipper as we learnt
in the city lessons; wrist turning it like the key in the door
to your house, where the fern is trained
along the bathroom wall, and the black cat stays;
where I am singing some of the old love songs
to eager new ears,
and the Ovation does not stand.

Jessica Peart

Jessica has run a number of readings and open mics around Dublin. Her work has appeared in journals. The following three poems are from Jessica.

Bargain Basement

The box of damp fliers I found
clearing out the shop basement
is so you, my old fling.
How you used to think no-one
would listen if you let loose,
so you held your breath
in an elastic band
fading and taught
as noose rope or
a string of thoughts
going nowhere,
stacked in a cardboard box
with the bottom falling out
on to the slab floor.
You, luckily, were top of the pile,
perfectly saved in water curves
wide as the last ripple escape.
Curled up in the four flap top
of an open box, I take you up
my stagnant eau de man,
best so long before,
now flat and creased
around the waist,
still advertising something
irrelevant, nevertheless,
selling ice to Inuits.
Posing limp to turn me on,
harping on you lost yourself
somewhere in Camus' *The Plague*,
existing just to entertain...
Well *I'll go on*, feck it,
from the basement to the attic,
stamping my identity mark
on the stairway,
tempted by banisters

back to your void self
steeped in old glory
and the musty heyday
of a smoker's kiss.
I'm not lit what with
cave drops of saliva
making our flicker
sail over my head
like a lie I know.
I rode the prism flame
centripetal wise to you,
sucked in like elastic
snapped by your eye
welling wick hot with love,
earth stores of groundwater -
got lost in your gravity as
you trickled away from me,
and your centre stage
and rock solid girl
to loose yourself artistically
between the paves in
New York Boogie Woogie
style, saturated and sinister
as your bright labyrinthine trace.
I picked up on your trail
just to blow you out, off,
from the palm of my hand
and any paths of Fortune
and sense left upstairs,
to let you flap your damp wings

so you can sell your wares elsewhere.

Sea shapes

I think I'll put my best dress on.
This curtain here is a tone weight
and has me drowned in material,
once I pulled the plug on that ship.

My dancing A-line dress is a blur,
a heaving corner of oil-slick.
slobbering up tall and white
and high on weed and family crest,
as celebrity nouveau riches
fished in for a pulse check
to feel if or perhaps not
I know anything but how to dress
To go swimmingly with everything.

So take my two arms out straight,
And give me stitches to pull
from bargain bins,
to wash, dry and hang on the line.
slapping and wrecking me still
wet behind the ears
as slips of the tongue
are innocent and true
as resurrected pearl
from precious, clammed jaw shell
and ghost ships' engines
twirling me cog-like
through figures of speech
and tired old dance steps
in the dress of an Empress
that sinks and pulls and
second-hand shakes me
air and kite dry all daylight.

Even

I am a womanly shaped
glass weight,
falling out in wide curves,
and champ on apple blossom
for Adam and I
to nest from head to toe
like one worms in tequila.

Ray Pospisil

Ray Pospisil, a Brooklyn poet and journalist, was born in Bogota, Colombia, and early in his life moved with his parents to Union, New Jersey. He spent most of his life in New York City. Ray's poems, which he often read for audiences in the East Village and elsewhere in Manhattan, were intensely personal, filled with vivid imagery and ranging from the humorous to the harrowing. His work has been published by *Lyric, Iambs & Trochees, The Newport Review, Rogue Scholars* and others. In 2006, his chapbook of poems, *Some Time Before the Bell*, was published by Modern Metrics Press. A collection of his work, *The Bell,* will be published by Seven Towers in 2009. Ray died tragically in January 2008. The following three poems are by Ray.

Insomnia

Some radios on call-in stations buzzed
and crackled underneath my bed at night,
preventing me from sleeping. As I tossed
to find a posture that would shut them out
and let me sleep at least an hour, the buzz
began congealing into words I heard.
But all the voices ranted on their harsh
obsessive paths of snide hysteria,
contemptuously barking down the ones
who called. And gradually they harmonized
till everyone was talking all the same,
but throwing echoes like you get around
a baseball park when radios throughout
the stands all blare the same announcer's voice,
announcer's voice,

                  with just a slight delay
a slight delay

          from those that stretch out through
the distance,

         through the distance

                  of the packed
and restless crowd. I gripped the sheets, and as
the voices came together they emerged
from underneath my bed as holograms
of heads that rose above me. They were stern
and never blinked. They hung there silently.
And then one spoke, repeated by the rest
in staggered sequence like the rounds in songs
for kids. "You will succeed.

                You will succeed
in crushing spirits,

          crushing spirits.

                Those
around you will be damaged by your good
intentions,

        good intentions,

              just the way
it's always been,

        it's always been

            your good

intentions. All the precious dreams you now
can bring to sweet fruition,
                            you can bring
      to sweet fruition
                        after years of work
and struggle, will indeed come true,
                                  indeed
come true,
            · *by years of work and struggle.*
                                        But
the dreams will turn to what you're suffering now
though ten times worse than this,
                                you're suffering now
      though ten times worse.
                              You'll feel you've chased a dim
elusive ghost and when you finally grasp
a hold, it burns like steam,
                        elusive ghost,
and when you finally grasp a hold it burns
and dissipates,
                  elusive ghost,
                        it burns
      like steam,
                  elusive ghost,
                                  and dissipates
in air.
            You will be lonely growing old
but you will always have consoling hope
of true self-realization
                        growing old
you will be lonely with consoling hope
of true self-realization in a bleached,
locked ward
                  creating realization in
      a bleached, locked ward
                              creating moccasins."

The first head stopped and licked its lips as all
the other heads' cascading echoes closed
that final cadence, one by one, and fell
to silence, hissing on the "moccasins."

I thought the heads would fade and let me sleep,
but they continued pulsing, shimmering
reflections of the green electric glow
my bedside clock emitted—3:09.
And then the first head spoke again: "There is
a way for you to show some courage now,
to compensate for all the harm and all
the disappointment your pathetic deeds
of goodness have inflicted on the world.
It's in your hands to leave the world a kind
of legacy"
                    —and all the other heads
joined in—
                    "Your absence."
                              Then the first one spoke
alone. "Bequeath your absence, which will carve
a space for light where only shadow looms."
I started getting up but then he spoke
again. "Be grateful for the shit you'll miss:
the riots over gasoline, the floods
from polar ice caps melting, wars and bombs,
and mobs arousing people from their beds
at night for quick tribunals, marched away
for execution, confiscating hearts
and eyes and kidneys for the auction trade.
Be glad you'll miss it, count your blessings." All
the other heads agreed and nodded "yes"
in unison.
              "You've got a chance to grab
your fate, so be pro-active, close the deal,
and never let them say again you lacked
the traits of character that leaders show."

I leaped up from the bed and threw a punch
but all the heads dispersed in glowing smoke.
I did a hundred jumping jacks and drank
a couple beers, a shot of vodka, then
another till my nerves began to calm,

until my nerves began to calm.
                                    A shot
of vodka till my nerves relaxed.
                                        I tried
to mute the echoes with a cable show
on offshore drilling,
                        drilling through the sea
to punch a hole into the crust of earth.
I wondered why the ocean doesn't all
run down the hole into the molten core
and turn to steam, and rise up through the cracks
in streets and cellar floors. We'll heat our homes
while cars with little vacuum cleaners suck
it up to move their pistons. Power plants
could draw it through their turbine blades to spin
all day. We'll never have to drill again.
We'll never have to drill a rolling sea
arrayed before the light when everyone
is warm and all the wars have ended, all
the pretty sea is warm and all the fish
are thriving, and we never have to drill
again while everyone is warm and all
the fish arrayed before us shine, and all
the turbines turn and all the cars run on
in silence through the pretty sea where all
the fish are rolling and the wars are done.

Subway Crash

For an instant after I heard the crash,
before I hit the rail of the seat,
breaking my rib cage,
I had this magnificent feeling of balance.
My feet were really still on the floor
but my weight was rising . . .

Now as they're lifting me onto a stretcher,
EMS crews triaging victims,
cops hauling metal cylinders in,
and firemen spraying foam on debris,
I only remember that feeling of balance.

My feet were really still on the floor
but my weight was rising, rising,
and all I heard was a tune in my head,
which flowed into the voice of a woman screaming
(I could see her fillings)
and the pop-eyed look on a guy arched backwards,
feet in the air
as purses, iPods, attachés and Gameboys
flew across the car amid the fluttering papers
and smashed against the poles and windows . . .
Foot pain? . . . 1-800-LAWYERS . . . For special evenings only. . .
If you see something say something . . . Budweiser,
Doublemint, lights, plaid, plastic seat rushing up to my face . . .

And as the door of the ambulance slams
I only remember that feeling of balance.
My weight is really still on the ground
but I'm rising, rising, rising . . .

Spite

It's odd we bottle spite so long
and feed on slights from years ago –
a kind of fuel that makes you strong
to grab authority and show

the bastards. Strange, however much
we burn, we've always got enough
supply. So go explode a batch
of spite. But even if you stuff

it down for years, it will emerge
in lust, or dice, or coke, a shove
for wealth, a tidy house, an urge
to drink or get the world to love

your face – and still the fuel gauge peaks
at full. Our scientists should learn
the secret, making OPEC sheiks
all fear this hot, undying burn.

Raven

Raven hails from San Francisco. A mesmeric live poet at the very top of his game who has shared the stage with the very best, including American poet Saul Williams, the world's premier live literature and spoken word artist. Raven is a native Californian and perfected his skill at the seminal Sacred Grounds Poetry, San Francisco immediately prior to relocating to Dublin in May 2005. The following three poems are by Raven.

Midway

The conceit of our youth:
a barker's testifying from sideshow pulpits
riling heat under illustrated eaves, lustrous leaves
exalting summer's spectacle
and the eager part taken in our own deceit.

White dewy mouths of lilies, futilely gilded,
fretful bulbs cloistered in urgency,
the lotus in her guile and repose
and the day's eye blindsided
following the sun
in kissing her hands, white petals
I have never known so well,
beckoning to transient abodes –
the drone on the midway the same in the meadow

which carried away in passing
our ageless shape and shade
and, moving on laden
with our dust thus scattered
over fertile years,
along unfollowable paths,
guaranteed sanctity
to the vanity of bonfires at the short endS of days
with this moment's despair:

why does the bee suck from the flower
if not for the flower's pleasure too?

when too soon it comes, and with turning
leaves
skeletal rods wind down, cease cranking
dervish facets release their hold,
the rush of the calliope
slowed in a humid air
and the breathless blur of the carousel
coalesced into paler faces awake and left behind by revelry;
bulleting through funhouse mirrors
one last time,
a regret moving faster than the diminishing days

no sleep but resleep
every birth in transition along a highwire
irrefutably anchored from end to end,
tense, finite and done.
In later hours, on longer nights –
smoke, the tally and shares.
Fire eaters shoot hooch,
fortune tellers divine the mundane
from daily papers
and rubber men buy liniment,
stretch limbs into withering reason,
blossoms,
pavilions collapse
leave no debt to past residence.

Buffalo Shoot

She is a social animal
that grazes in the plains
and listens
and knows what you would never guess
that grass is not mute
even when uprooted and chewed to a pulp
its dialogue with her is plaintive
asking
how old is the world
which is only this plain
this spot in her shade
this single blade
pulled from this life
we are all lifted in succession
with the same lack of concern
and the same love
we never know she is gone
even when crushed by her weight
a bullet from a passing train is not in our
vocabulary of life
that bends and submits and wakes up
after storms have walked through
and still thrives
she could be sleeping, for all we know.

Moving Cities

If we are lucky
we will
pull our bodies in time
from the wreckage
of architecture
moving cities will
only collide
moving people meet
we will go without windows
to press longing
faces against
or walls
to hang empty
devotions from
homes go rushing blind
empties of compassion
full of light and belongings
only the burdens of discomfort
only the sounds of
passing feet.

Oran Ryan

Oran is a novelist, short story writer, poet, playwright and screenwriter from Dublin. His first two novels *The Death of Finn* and *Ten Short Novels by Arthur Kruger* were published by Seven Towers in 2006. In 2008 Oran won an Arts Council bursary for his current work in progress *New Order from Zero,* a novel in three volumes. The following haiku and short story are by Oran.

Dead man walking

On dead ecstasy streets
Angels take me away
With my songs

Climb down

Like pigeons
Trapped in the attic of dreams
Take wing

Remember

Only great love
Forgotten
Brings the doom

Some day

The bullet's approach
The world's tears
Cannot stop my songs

Train to Dublin

The tracks are waiting
Horizons open
But no train

Chisty is Dead

The child I am
Is gone
In this song

Cheers

Smile, friend
Between your glass and mine
We have time

Don't Lie

Lovers turn
To each other
Then see the truth

The Critic

The sniper's crosshairs
The spinning bullet
Bores me

Civil Service

In Dracula's thrall
One never tries in vein
Forever a child of night

The most fun Dromedary Orwell ever had

Was not when he was younger and even more stupid, tried and succeeded to emergency operate on a twelve year old appendicitis patient while high on Xanax, nor when he used to dissect foetal guinea pigs or, with a hypersharp paper slicer, pop out the eyes of corpses in one deft pluck as a kind of late night dissection room party trick, or on a less cutting motif, seduce nurses already in committed relationships as an intern during clinic duty (they had to be at least three years with the same person, extra points if she was in love with another woman), nor when he used hack into his bosses' mail accounts as a personal insurance against being fired, getting past the spies and trawlers and sniffers and harvesters and spiders and see into the words, taking down all relevant data, interdepartmental communiqués on policy and personnel, hints and proof of corruption and affairs and these were the times and this was the why Orwell never got fired, never failed an exam, remained the good son to his father and mother, twin doctors one a gynaecologist the other a thoracic surgeon who in the end got him a regular practice downtown upstairs in a hyper eighty acre shopping mall where a few came and went and over time, enabling him to build up a semi regular clientele. Dromedary managed to pose as a regular guy cause he was no such thing and he knew it how he knew it, because he made it clear he would bring down as many of those in authority he could if they took any official sanction against him and this was why he was never censured as an utter incompetent by the Irish Medical Organization, why his self absorbed disruptive life coasted along as the lives of most professional incompetents coasted along; never really challenging himself, never really trying to understand the great weight of emptiness he carried inside himself; never really trying to connect with others, never really feeling regret or guilt or using his gifts or finding that primordial focus that would release that dark boredom and frustration he felt at existing at all, reading when he should be working, getting stoned or drunk when he should be fully present, addicting himself to whatever pleasures he allowed himself to feel, knowing he felt the pain of pleasure because underneath the pleasure there lay nothing rage hate love nothing, marrying because one married at a certain point, learning deeply the fine art of politicking as a compensation for feeling crippling mediocrity, and most of all, always making sure he got paid, which was quite the feat of accounting, not declaring certain monies while at the same time fully declaring others, death and taxes being at the end of all pleasure. No, none of this was real fun, the most fun he ever had was the afternoons he spent replying to emails from people he never knew, people who tried to scam him by making him or whoever else was stupid enough to reply to them by giving their bank account details so that the sender of the electronic mail could empty that account or use it as a means to funnel cash from one account to another for the purposes of laundering the money. That was fucking fun. So he couldn't get a job in a hospital, couldn't get work in any reputable institution, not even with all his connections, which enraged and depressed him, spent his days reading, taking drugs, and answering emails from people he never knew. Dear sir dear kind sir I wonder if you can help me please. My father President Aideril Z. Zambesa, President of the People's Republic of Luyaire, has been wrongly imprisoned and horribly tortured for many years as the father of the people's liberation in my home country I hope you do not find this unsolicited email too forward but the situation in my country has become intolerable for the many suffering peoples who have endured so much poverty and injustice and exploitation on the part of ruthless imperialist nations who have taken everything from my people, their dignity their hope of a better future, infrastructures and hospitals. Ours is a war torn country and we need help, help that established nations will not give simply because the corrupt government in power using torture and death squads gives special assistance to powerful nations in the guise of essential raw materials. We are in a desperate situation here. Soon our neighbouring countries will invade us, these powerful nations I already mentioned will intervene, and the last hope for a democracy will fade. I have a very substantial sum of monies in legitimate currencies, many different currencies, that I wish to put into a legitimate holding account so we can use this money, which belongs to my father fully and completely and was obtained I might add in a completely moral and ethical Christian manner. If there was a way I could contact you so that we could talk about this matter further I would be immensely grateful may god and his blessed mother bless you kind regards Kathy Z. Zambesa, daughter to the rightful president of the People's Republic of Luyaire. And Dromedary, checking the electronic mail really did originate from the aforementioned country, tickled at the prose and inconsistent argument in the mail, wrote Dear Kathy, I was so moved by the terrible plight of you and your father and it really made me think. I have engaged in considerable research into your situation and alerted some friends in the Irish Department of Foreign Affairs and we are prepared to offer you and your father, who is to my mind the rightful President of Luyaire, a beautiful country by the way Kathy, I spent some time in Luyaire some years ago, a country full of richness and many many natural resources, some form of substantial relief. I would ask you to please respond to this email and let us try to set up some kind of mechanism so that we understand each other fully and know how to proceed. With kindest regards, Dr Dromedary Orwell, MD GP. The response to this mail was understandably slow. Approximately ninety percent of those soliciting account numbers usually never responded to this particular email Orwell sent, giving credence to the sender's plight, while at the same time challenging some of their fundamental arguments about their situation and implicit request for assistance. Weeks passed during which the number of regular patients to the doctor's waiting rooms grew pitifully fewer, a couple in the morning and one or two flu sufferers or heart patients later on in the day. We're gonna die anyway, Drommy thought. Dromedary disliked house calls, as he disliked cats and his parents, but house calls were a good source of revenue, and also he got to see the interiors of other's houses, something that was of interest to him, enabling to him to profile the types of personalities who lived there and especially if such families were useful to him as future high profile connections. Over the years he was able to make connections firstly in the music industry by being on call for gigs and concerts, turning up at four in the morning to help someone detox or give an essential band member a maintenance shot or a flu jab or something to keep a star from burning out in the middle of a crushingly difficult tour. He didn't want this, but it was a living. He found himself being surly with actors and agents and artists, pointing out the absurdity of wanting to feel good while at the same time persisting in a self destructive lifestyle and occasionally these well received challenges led to his word being to a greater or lesser extent trusted and this led to a crossover into the other arts forms, painting, writing for cinema and even a few sculptors. He did like visiting the homes of sculptors, especially if they had talent. This was because experience taught him sculpture seemed to attract so many types; one could meet anyone there, even higher civil servants and the occasional ministers, potential needy patients who needed prescribed medication not normally obtainable without considerable reference to an established carefully regulated system on a government database that could leak into the media and ruin a reputation, which he enjoyed and gave him easy access to sex and drugs and in exchange for his strict silence, protection and peace of mind, that is until Kathy whatshername decides to write back Dear Doctor it is truly good to hear from you if you would care to check our credentials if that is what you want my passport number is ASDT 67009987733 LUY/1 obtained and renewed just last year through some government contact we have re routed and encrypted this particular email, making it difficult for those who would seek to harm us from seeing its true content. I wish to make it clear and we have also gone to the trouble of checking that you are a legitimate practitioner and all indications lead us to believe you are of excellent reputation and I thank you once again for taking the trouble to responding to us. As I indicated before we need access to an account number, not necessarily one you might regularly use, but one not used by you for some time, perhaps one from your youth. This would serve the purpose of spreading the monies as a far and wide as possible. You understand the need for this. We would need full electronic access to this account, and perhaps your telephone number as we would need to contact you in person. If you still feel uncomfortable with this arrangement, don't hesitate to decline response to this communication, which of course made the whole drama of it all irresistible to Doctor Drommy who wrote back to her saying dear Kathy my number is as follows four nine six five eight six six three, extension five six six and Kathy, that's a Dublin number, so because it's a Dublin number, you need to put the following digits before the number, that's zero three five three one, then put in the number I have given you. Looking forward to hearing from you during business hours and don't forget the time differential between your locale and mine kind regards Dromedary. Each morning Drommy arrived waiting with tingling fingertips for the call, took patients, waited, took drugs, read books, waited and waited for the call to come, tried to find distractions, waiting for the call to come but it never did and he stopped caring, until one night he was lounging at a club and his phone kept vibrating as the multicoloured fractals lights glimmering off the purple and cerulean roof kept depicting themselves in chimerical forms due to the lysergic acid and just the tinniest scintilla of methamphetamines and he heard the phone vibrate and continue to vibrate for fifteen minutes and then he answered it and said yes yes? Who is this? What? Huh? You are going to have to speak up, I'm at a...I'm at a party! Hi? Yes? Yes? This is who is this? This is Kathy! Kathy said, I am calling you from Luxembourg and then Dr Dromedary Orwell blanched and disconnected the call and switched off his phone and went home with a model actress whatever, whose name she said was Mary Lou, and she was doing a commercial the very next week and she would be appearing in the magazine Crispy Bits next month and as they had sex Drommy thought about Kathy and thought about his wife who was very pregnant and wondered if Kathy or indeed his wife really were ringing from Luxembourg and what the hell was really going on and the following morning at about five o clock he struggled home and had a long hot shower and long hot coffee and toast and sat at the edge of his bed and saw his wife was still asleep and he switched on his phone and tried to call the number back and got hotel reception and asked the location of the hotel. The number he had received the call from really was Luxembourg. He went to work and there sitting in his waiting office was a man who handed him his identification. His name was Joe Hammett and Joe Hammett a quiet spoken slightly pompous man in a perfect suit said he worked for the tax revenue offices. Had he, Dromedary Orwell, perhaps taken cognizance of the letters and phone calls and communiqués from Mr Hammett's superior's offices? Would he perhaps care to answer the following questions regarding his tax returns? And then Hammett as he sat in Drommys empty outer offices asked him a series of questions about his net incomes from any home visitations, being an oncall doctor for various music tours that had occurred throughout the last year and the differential between what had been declared by those tour accountants and those other individuals who had written up considerably larger sum of monies spent on doctors calling to the house over a period of months than Drommy had declared. Now the good doctor knew the tax man had no real proof of tax evasion rather than tax avoidance, that the sums spoken of in the list of questions were tiny, and that he, Drommy, needed to be ripping the tax off for at least ten times the amount under discussion there for them to really bother and really pursue him in the relentless terminator manner they pursued real criminals and then Drommy smiled and took out a cheque book and wrote a cheque for ten thousand and gave it to Hammett and said will that do the trick? And Hammett smiled and just then the phone rang and Dromedary put his hand up and said listen I have to take this call it's important even though he had no idea who it was because he hadn't bothered to look at the caller identification readout but it turned out it was Kathy and Kathy was crying, why she called out, why didn't you take my call my father is gone missing? Why did you not call me back and Hammett looked concerned. Is everything all right Dr Orwell? He asked? Everything? Just fine, Dromedary answered. Everything is fine, it's a crank call. I keep getting them in my office. Hold on a second and I will get rid of it. Listen Kathy, how are you? I have told you I am not good. My father is gone missing and I think he might be in real danger. I have informed Interpol but they are doing everything they can. I think I am being watched I am going to the Irish embassy over here but I really need that account numbers, Dr Dromedary. Can you give me them no please I beg you. That's no problem at all

Kathy I will give you them right now. Just hold on a second. And Dromedary Orwell put down the receiver beside the patient files and the books he was reading and waited five seconds and then took up the receiver of the phone and he spoke into it and he said listen Kathy do you have a pen or a pencil handy, because I am happy to say I have those account numbers right here the numbers are as follows first the bank account sort code. Oh thank you Doctor you are a good man I have a pencil here I am ready. Good Kathy the sort code for the bank account number is. And then Dromedary Orwell hung up on Kathy Z Zambesa and smiled to Joe Hammett and said, well that's that, the most fun I ever had, will there be anything else? Can I expect any other queries from your offices Mr Hammett? I doubt it, Doctor Dromedary. Thank you, thank you Mr Hammett. It's okay Doctor, Mr Hammett gestured, I will let myself out.

Good, that's great, listen; send in the next patient, will you?

John W Sexton

John W. Sexton is the author of three collections of poetry, *The Prince's Brief Career*, (*Cairn Mountain Press, 1995*), *Shadows Bloom / Scáthanna Faoi Bhláth*, a book of haiku with translations into Irish by Gabriel Rosenstock, and most recently *Vortex* (Doghouse, 2005). He has also written two novels for children, *The Johnny Coffin Diaries* and *Johnny Coffin School-Dazed*, both published by The O'Brien Press, which have been translated into Italian and Serbian. Under the ironic pseudonym of Sex W. Johnston he has recorded an album with legendary Stranglers frontman, Hugh Cornwell, entitled *Sons Of Shiva*, which has been released on Track Records. His poem *The Green Owl* was awarded the Listowel Poetry Prize 2007 for best single poem, and in the same year he was endowed with a Patrick and Katherine Kavanagh Fellowship in Poetry. The following three poems are by John.

A Japanese Airman Says Goodbye To The War

In the garden   chimes of slices of shell
conjure a song   from the wind.
Amongst the leaves   and fallen blossom
a snail displays   its two-pronged crown.

Mount Fuji   is nothing to this snail
who likewise   is nothing to me.

Your black hair   seems unbearably pure.
I take a tear   as a keepsake.
My plane is screaming   with tongues of fire
but the sea holds me   in its gaze.

seven eyes nine eyes twelve

lamprey mouth their language of scars
seven eyes nine eyes twelve
tissued flesh their face of knives
seven eyes nine eyes twelve

lamps ray south their coinage of stars
seven eyes nine eyes twelve
lighthouse cyclops sheds its tears
seven eyes nine eyes twelve

lamps spray forth their carnage of shards
seven eyes nine eyes twelve
ships pass down through fathomless years
seven eyes nine eyes twelve

twenty-eight minimalist chapters from

the gizzard of was

(1) a fallen hair slices the earth

(2) plums rot into themselves in the garden of desperate measures

(3) none can shut tighter than marzipan doors

(4) ebony angel the electrical man is still on when he's off

(5) behind damp wallpaper silverfish eat the last binding paste

(6) omens in elephant dung the clowns take their leave of the circus

(7) mother sets a fire in our existential house of ice

(8) whose mind in the owl's mind whose

(9) noun one the legless larva of a fly two slang for margaret

(10) brassica walking stick sprouts in his sleep

(11) his colon rotted punctuation artuad shits in a bag

(12) slumbering keats all cold in his sedge pyjamas

(13) o emptiness of this empty vase my emptiness

(14) on the stairway stars burn holes in her hair as he shakes his head no

(15) we kiss the shape of your face soft in the winding sheet

(16) mengele places israel into a woven basket of skin and hair

(17) king nadir your toadstool palace bloats out

(18) via grave beetle to kingdom come

(19) three mice with muddy eyes preserve prosody for good

(20) christ's risen chassis pranged on route 66

(21) seen in the nihilist's anti mirror an ism of no is yes

(22) neinsteins say the rhythmic evolving universe merely white noise

(23) where your breath of fire bakes glass castles

(24) drizzle melts the chalked shape of a murdered son

(25) gin mind or zen mind the gutter is constant

(26) snails on the pages of cabbage his name written in slime

(27) in every sound egg the whites are in the dark

(28) mojocycle a vibrant skull on the moth's back

Eileen Sheehan

Eileen Sheehan is from Scartaglin, County Kerry; now living in Killarney. Her first collection, *Song of the Midnight Fox* was published in 2004 and her second collection *Down the Sunlit Hall* was published in 2008, both by Doghouse. Winner of the inaugural Writers' Week Listowel, Poetry Slam, 2004 and the Brendan Kennelly Poetry Award 2006. She is on the Poetry Ireland Éigse Éireann Writers in Schools Scheme and has been employed by County Kerry VEC teaching Creative Writing at Killarney Technical College. In April 2008 she read at The National American Conference for Irish Studies at St Ambrose University, Iowa, USA. She is currently Poet in Residence for Limerick County. The following three poems are by Eileen.

Threat of Rain

When we sit with our dead
for a day and a night

we share their death for a while

we take on their stillness
their absolute quiet
      a calm place to be
      for a day and a night

then we take on their journey
take their weight
on our shoulders

to the very edge of the grave
we travel with them

but we don't go down

we measure the sky
the moving clouds
the threat of rain

we step back
at the sound of earth on wood
      back to notice the living

      back into our own
      diminished lives

Songbird in the House

Startling to a child
how the sparrow flew
through the kitchen door
and swooped inside the neckline
of my mother's dress.

It drew the breath from her.
She whispered, *Oh,*
I can feel its heart going mad
Against my own.

It was said that a songbird in the house
was a harbinger of death for someone there

she claimed it was only a small soul
gone astray
and meant no harm to anyone.

My mother,
a young woman then,
stepped outside,
loosed the string
on her cross-over bib,

let the frantic creature go
into the waiting sky

In Conversation With My Father

In dreams, the dead
are no less real
than the living

although sometimes I say to my father,
when he strolls across the acre,
you're dead, you can't be here.
He tells me, *whisht,*
as if such trivia
isn't important there.
He tells me, *listen.*

He continues to walk towards me
real as the grass I am dreaming;
real as the warm breeze;
as the sycamore tree
in the corner. Real
as the thrush on the branch,

real as the thrush-song
I hear as I'm waking.

The song bids me *whisht.*
 It bids me to *listen.*

Barbara Smith

Barbara Smith is a native of Armagh and currently lives in Dundalk, County Louth where she teaches creative writing. Barbara has also been involved in amateur dramatics, various writing groups and worked with the Irish Mental Health Association in the organisation of a short story competition. Barbara has published poetry in *Riposte, VirtualWriter and Electric Acorn* in Ireland, as well as in *nthposition.com, Sentinel Poetry* (online) and *The Coffee House* (UK), *Garm Lu* (Canada), *Borderlands: Texas Poetry Review* and *Portrait* (US) and *TMR* (India). Her essays have appeared in *west47* online and *VirtualWriter* and her publications include *Poetic Stage* (1998) and *Gnosis* (1996). Her collection *Kairos* was published by Doghouse in 2007. Of the three poems by Barbara that follow, *Feeding the Calves* was selected for the August 2007, Guardian Poetry Workshop, facilitated by Matthew Sweeney; first line from a poem by W. S. Graham.

The Garden of Earthly Delights

In the kitchen, Valentine,
it will begin, with the green
curlicues of garlic shoots hid
in the cold shelf of the fridge.

The prying, bulging eyes of spuds
will wink in the clammy closeness
of their plastic bag. All being pulled
spring tight tonight, through the tilting

built into their bolting seed husks.
And you too will respond, with the flick
in your loins, the click in your head
as my hands riot in the radishes,

tease out the aubergine chunks,
toss together pillows of cherry tomatoes
and delight in these firm ruins
of last year's seedpods. There,

Valentine, is where you will begin.

Feeding the Calves

I have my yellow boots on to walk
beside your greater, green ones.
Our feet squidge, splodge across
the mud mouth of the shed gate
where the calves tread their own muck
and the straw into an earthen brown
pocked with their cloven prints.
Even the rain has given up this winter,
the insistent chill invading my red anorak.
'We have wind from the North,' you mutter.
*'That means snow and more blessed
misery.'* You pour the calf nuts
into the clang of the metal feeder.
The smell of warm tea oozes from them;
their breath steaming, as the calves
nudge their heads through the bars,
warm in themselves

Misunderstood Second Wife

This morning, I am ready if you are,
to take back the words I flung at you.
They were hasty, I said things to hurt you
that would needle you, press the right buttons.
I was looking for BBC 1 - but
you gave a bravura Channel 4;
There were your days, stolen, drunk at some bar,
rejecting my calls when I rang you,
or the granules when I wanted powder.
But the best one of all is this last one,

when the barbs hooked you and stuck in your flesh:
your long strides to the front door, a crash
the door frame juddered, the car door smashed shut
and your dinner followed on the windscreen.

First line from a poem by W. S. Graham.

Patricia Walsh

Patricia lives in Cork and is a regular contributor to the open mic at Ó Bhéal. The following two poems are by Patricia.

Winter Evening

Do sit down. I cannot find
Words or time to describe you.
Make yourself some tea, sit down
By the carriage clock that sings the hour.

How do I know you? *Gach lá,*
I see the finer points refined
To extinction. Beauty never lasts long
Enough to appreciate its vainglory.

I love you so much it hurts. As you remain
By the fire alone I see the blood
Between us rise and overflow.
Don't make a scene, just relax.

Rest with me awhile. The winter sunset
Grapples for attention with the stars.
Switch off the sun, let us rise
To occasions where nothing is demanded.

Indiscretion

Kiss me, while the day still is.
Night will surely follow, and then
We won't know what to do with ourselves.
Kiss me, while I feel slightly awkward
Enough to make you calm me through.
Night will surely follow, and the
The dark will thunder through faith and reason
Enough to make us break ranks with our senses.
Kiss me, while there is light outside.
I need to walk home and the sodium lights
Don't offer quite the same protection.
Night will surely follow and then
I will be left with more than a thought of you.
And when I rise my heart will be full
To shining through the small hours
As it does in Norway, for I can never contain

The consequence you have for me.

Doog Wood

Doog Wood is from North Carolina and now lives in Dublin, where he teaches. His work has been published in a number of anthologies and Doog has taken part in readings on both sides of the Atlantic. His first collection will be published by Seven Towers in Spring 2009. The following three poems are by Doog.

Dr. Maglure

Dr. Maglure rode atop the old mailcar
one early winter morning through the pine
with a black hat, suit, and cold eye tucked
behind his dusty coat pocket like the watch
of a hard-down straw boss, and he smelled
like a horse. Course, we figured men smelled
like horses and whiskey, and the only thing
different about Maglure was people called
him "Doctor" and somehow that made him
                    the fattest man I'd seen.

I wondered if folks said "Doctor" enough
it might make us all fat and whether that
meant really eating well or just breathing
heavy and needing a cane to keep your fat legs
walking, seemed we all wanted to be fat
just a little. Cause for those five or ten minutes
however long it took Maglure to get
from the mailcar into our house we almost
                    forgot Helen was dying.

Dished

I made hit well of seasoned oak:
back wheels cut, wood chisel
& half-inch slope on one side –
more and more weight
will strengthen th'spokes instead
of bowing out. I call hit 'dished.'
Too many riding sloped ground.
So the spokes is 'dished'
Outward, split apart.

23

I can smell good cigars, shirt-sleeved men
'stay, . . . here I'll git in,' so I sit
looking
at shirt-sleeved men, back and forth
back   & forth, and the cart outside
a cowshed.

Two dogs came back, they drink from th'wheel
one, worn-out, straightens again –
beside me
the shirt-sleeves men, laughs, then
drinks a sip of corn parched coffee
from a tin.

She rises, thrusting her head, like human
and there's a chain, 'Esco, haint you ready,'
shirtsleeves
laughs and spits, 'in a couple days now,'
th'signboard passes, & she smells good
like good cigars, and coffee.